S0-BPI-174

Thomas Reid on
Freedom and Morality

Also by William L. Rowe

The Cosmological Argument

Philosophy of Religion: An Introduction

Philosophy of Religion: Selected Readings (coedited with William Wainwright)

Religious Symbols and God: A Philosophical Study of Tillich's Theology

William L. Rowe

Thomas Reid on Freedom and Morality

Cornell University Press

Ithaca and London

First published 1991 by Cornell University Press.

International Standard Book Number 0-8014-2557-3
Library of Congress Catalog Card Number 90-55715
Printed in the United States of America
Librarians: Library of Congress cataloging information appears on the last page of the book.

∞ The paper in this book meets the minimum requirements of the American National Standard for Information Sciences—Permanence of Paper for Printed Library Materials, ANSI Z39.48-1984.

For George Nakhnikian

Contents

Preface

I became interested in the eighteenth-century controversy over freedom and necessity some years ago while completing a study of the Cosmological Argument, particularly as presented by Samuel Clarke. In the course of reviewing Clarke's work, I happened upon and read with interest his polemic in defense of libertarian freedom against the well-known attack by Anthony Collins. It was not until I later read Reid's *Essays on the Active Powers of the Human Mind,* however, that I began to understand fully the metaphysical roots of libertarian freedom in the idea that human beings are agents with active power, capable of being genuine causes of changes in themselves and other things. It was also Reid who stressed the importance of *moral liberty,* liberty conjoined with practical reason judging what we morally ought to do or what is for our long-range good. It struck me that Reid's work in defense of libertarian freedom was first-rate, fully deserving careful study by contemporary philosophers. My hope is that this book will help the reader appreciate what I believe are Reid's important contributions to the controversy over freedom and necessity.

My research for the early portion of this book was supported by a grant from the Guggenheim Foundation and from the National Humanities Center. The Institute for Advanced Studies of the University of Edinburgh and the Center for Humanistic Studies at Purdue University provided valuable assistance while I was completing the final draft of the manuscript. I am also indebted to the National Endowment for the Humanities for a travel grant to use the research facilities of the University of Edinburgh.

Several of my colleagues at Purdue University provided me with helpful comments on some of the philosophical problems with which the book deals. Special thanks are due to Rod Bertolet, who read and commented on the entire manuscript. I am also indebted to David Widerker for helpful discussions on the topic of free will.

Permission has been granted to use material from the following previously published articles and addresses: "Causality and Free Will in the Controversy between Collins and Clarke," *Journal of the History of Philosophy* 25 (1987): 51–67; "Reid's Conception of Human Freedom," *The Monist* 70 (1987): 430–41; "Two Concepts of Freedom" (Presidential Address, Central Division), *Proceedings and Addresses of the APA* 61 (1987): 43–64; "Responsibility, Agent-Causation and Freedom: An Eighteenth-Century View," *Ethics* 101 (1991): 270–97.

WILLIAM L. ROWE

West Lafayette, Indiana

Thomas Reid on
Freedom and Morality

I

Background: Locke's Conception of Freedom

For how can we think any one freer than to have the power to do what we will.

—John Locke

In his chapter on power in *An Essay Concerning Human Understanding,* John Locke (1632–1704) characterized freedom (liberty) as "the power a man has to do or forbear doing any particular action according . . . as he himself wills it."[1] Before we look with care at Locke's conception of freedom, it is helpful to note that he and the other eighteenth-century participants in the controversy over freedom and necessity all embraced what has come to be known as the volitional theory of action. Since this theory is common to the participants in the controversy we are examining, it plays no significant role in the controversy itself. Nevertheless, some brief description of it will help us understand certain points that emerge in the controversy.

According to this theory, actions are of two sorts: those that primarily involve thoughts and those that primarily involve motions of the body. What makes the occurrence of a certain thought or bodily motion an *action* is its being preceded by a certain act of will (a volition) which brings about the thought or motion. Volitions, then, are "action starters." On the other

1. *Essay,* book 2, chap. 21, sec. 15 (1st ed.).

hand, they are also themselves referred to as "actions." Of course, if we do classify volitions as actions, we cannot say that *every* action must be preceded by a volition. For then no action could occur unless it were preceded by an absolutely infinite number of volitions. But we still can say that thoughts and bodily motions are actions only if *they* are preceded by volitions that cause them. It is not clear whether volitions that start actions are viewed as distinct from the actions started, or as a part of the actions. It is also unclear just what the agent wills when his volition starts (or is part of) a certain action. These uncertainties, however, as important as they are, will have little bearing on our examination of the two conceptions of freedom (Locke's and Reid's) that dominated eighteenth-century thought.[2]

In setting forth his account of freedom Locke stresses that one is free (at liberty) with respect to an action A just in case one has *both* the power to do A should one will to do A *and* the power to refrain from doing A should one will to refrain: "where either of them [doing A; refraining from doing A] is not in the power of the agent to be produced by him according to his volition, there he is not at liberty; that agent is under necessity."[3] Locke's insistence that for your action in doing A to be free it must be that you could have refrained from doing A had you willed to refrain leads him to distinguish a *voluntary action* from a *free action.* For your action to be voluntary all that is required is that you will to do that action and perform it, presumably as a result of your willing to do it. For example, suppose you are sitting in your chair and someone invites you to go for a walk. You reject the idea, choosing instead to remain just where you are. Your so remaining, Locke would say, is a voluntary act. But was it a free

2. Although Reid's *Essays on the Active Powers of the Human Mind* did not appear until 1788, the conception of freedom he there elaborated and defended was not original with him. Samuel Clarke had put forth a similar view in the first decade of the century.

3. *Essay,* book 2, chap. 21, sec. 8.

act? This is a further question for Locke, and it depends on whether you could have done otherwise had you so willed. If I had injected you with a powerful drug, so that at the time—perhaps without your being aware of it—your legs were paralyzed, then your act of remaining in the chair was voluntary but not free, for you could not have got up and walked had you willed to do so. A free act, says Locke, is not just a voluntary act.[4] An act is free if it is voluntary *and* it is true that had you willed to refrain from doing it you would have been able to refrain. For Locke, then, we can say that you are free with respect to a certain action provided it is in your power to do it if you will to do it *and* in your power to refrain from doing it if you should will to refrain. Locke tells us that a person who is chained in prison does not stay in prison freely—even if that is what he wants to do—because it is not in his power to leave if he should will to leave. But if the prison doors are thrown open and his chains are removed, he is free to leave and free to stay for he can do either, depending on his will.

Locke's remarks invite us to distinguish a *free agent* and a *necessary agent* with respect to an action roughly as follows.

> S is a *free agent* with respect to action A just in case it is in S's power to do A should S will to do A and it is in S's power to refrain from doing A should S will to refrain from doing A.

> S is a *necessary agent* with respect to action A just in case either it is not in S's power to do A should S will to do A or it is not in S's power to refrain from doing A should S will to refrain from doing A.

4. Don Locke in "Three Concepts of Free Action" fails to see that John Locke distinguishes between a voluntary and a free act. Thus he wrongly interprets Locke as holding "that to act freely is to act as you want to: the man who wants to get out of a locked room does not remain there freely but, Locke insists, a man who wants to stay there, to speak to a friend, does stay freely, even if the door is locked." *Proceedings of the Aristotelian Society* supplementary volume 49 (1975): 95.

Given Locke's distinction between a free action and a voluntary action, it should be clear that an action of a necessary agent could be a voluntary action, but it cannot be a free action. For if the agent wills to do A and does A, his action is voluntary. But if it was not in his power to refrain from doing A had he willed to refrain, he is a necessary agent with respect to doing A. Necessity, in Locke's sense, is the opposite of free; the opposite of voluntary is not necessity but involuntary.[5]

There is, however, a second, more important sense of 'necessary agent' that we need to have before us. Anthony Collins (1676–1729), Locke's friend and follower, introduces this other sense in *A Philosophical Inquiry Concerning Human Liberty*. According to Collins a person is a necessary agent if the person's actions are so determined by the causes preceding each action that, given the causes and circumstances, no other action was possible.[6] Collins points out that a person may be both a necessary agent (in our second sense) and a free agent in Locke's sense. For on the assumption that a person's willing to do A is among the *causes* of her action of doing A, it may well be true that she is causally determined to do A and, therefore, given the causes, couldn't have refrained from doing A, and yet is such that she could have refrained from doing A *had she willed to refrain*. For had she willed to refrain the causes would have been different.

Collins argued that all our actions are subject to causal necessity; he argued, that is, that our actions are so determined by the causes preceding them that, given the causes and circumstances, no other actions were possible. What are the

5. *Essay*, book 2, chap. 21, sec. 11.

6. Collins's definition of 'necessary agent' is as follows. "Man is a *necessary Agent*, if all his actions are so determin'd by the causes preceding each action, that not one past action could possibly not have come to pass, or have been otherwise than it hath been; nor one future action can possibly not come to pass, or be otherwise than it shall be." *A Philosophical Inquiry Concerning Human Liberty* (London, 1717), 11. References are to the text as edited and annotated by J. O'Higgins: *Determinism and Freewill: Anthony Collins' A Philosophical Inquiry Concerning Human Liberty*.

causes of our actions? Well, the immediate cause of the action is your decision or act of will to perform that action. What is the cause of your making that decision? According to Locke and Collins, the cause of that act of will is your desires, judgments, and the circumstances that prevailed just prior to that decision. Given your desires and judgments at the time, and given the circumstances that prevailed, it was impossible for you not to will as you did. And given the desires, judgments, circumstances, and act of will, it was impossible for you not to act as you did. To re-emphasize the point made above, however, this impossibility of willing and acting otherwise does not conflict with Lockean freedom. For Lockean freedom does not require that *given the causes,* we somehow could have acted differently. All it requires is that *if* we had decided or willed differently *then* we could have acted differently. Indeed, Locke is careful to note that the absolute determination of the will or preference of the mind does not preclude freedom so far as the action flowing from the will or preference of the mind is concerned. He remarks:

> But though the preference of the mind be always determined . . . ; yet the person who has the power, in which alone consists liberty to act, or not to act, according to such preference, is nevertheless free; such determination abridges not that power. He that has his chains knocked off, and the prison doors set open to him, is perfectly at liberty, because he may either go or stay as he best likes; though his preference be determined to stay by the darkness of the night, or illness of the weather, or want of other lodging. He ceases not to be free; though that which at that time appears to him the greater good absolutely determines his preference, and *makes* him stay in his prison.[7]

Let us call those who believe both that we have Lockean freedom and that our actions and acts of will are subject to

7. *Essay,* book 2, chap. 21, sec. 33 (1st ed.).

causal necessity, *necessitarians.* It is likely that Locke was a necessitarian; Hobbes (1588–1679) and Collins most certainly were. Those who, like Clarke (1675–1729) and Reid (1710–1796), hold that necessity (in our second sense) and freedom are really inconsistent with one another do not disagree with the necessitarians concerning the consistency of *Lockean freedom* with the causal necessity of our actions and acts of will. What they reject is the whole notion of Lockean freedom. In its place they propose an altogether different conception of freedom and argue that freedom, as they conceive it, is inconsistent with the causal necessity of our acts of will. We will later examine this alternative conception of freedom. Before we consider the more salient objections to Lockean freedom, however, it will be helpful to consider what Locke has to say about freedom as it is applied to the will, as opposed to being applied to the actions that flow from our acts of will.

Thus far little or nothing has been said about the question of whether the will is free. And this was what Locke preferred, thinking on the whole that the question of freedom is the question of whether you are free *to do* what you will; much confusion, he thought, results from asking whether you are free *to will* what you will. But, of course, the question of whether we are free with respect to our acts of will could not be completely ignored. So, having set forth his conception of freedom (liberty)—a conception that applies to actions that follow upon volitions—Locke turned to consider what can be said with respect to freedom of the will itself. He considers three questions: (1) Is the will free? (2) Is the person free to will? (3) Does a person have freedom to will which of the two he pleases, motion or rest?

Locke rejects the first question as senseless. "It is plain then that the will is nothing but one power or ability, and freedom another power or ability so that, to ask, whether the will has freedom, is to ask whether one power has another power, one ability another ability; a question at first sight too grossly absurd to make a dispute, or need an answer."[8] The second question is intelligible but, on Locke's view, deserves a negative answer. In most cases, when an action that is in our power is proposed to us, we are not free whether to will or not will. For we must either will to do the action or will to refrain from doing the action. Moreover, if we treat the act of will as itself an *action* and ask whether it is free in Locke's sense, the act of will turns out to be free only if it is preceded by another act of will, and so on *ad infinitum.*[9] The third question is absurd, for it asks "whether a man can will what he wills, or be pleased with what he is pleased with?"[10]

Locke's responses to the first and third questions are fair enough, but his first response to the second question (Is the person free to will?) is rather contrived. His point is this. A person is free with respect to *acting* provided he can act (if he wills) and refrain from acting (if he wills). But when an action is under consideration by us, we are not free with respect to *willing* because we must either will to do the action or will to refrain from doing the action. We are free to act or not act, but we aren't free to will or not will.

What are we to make of this point concerning the necessity of willing when an action is proposed to us? First, it is worth noting that Locke is quite willing to count the *forbearance* of an action (movement or thought) as itself an action.

> To avoid multiplying of words, I would crave leave here, under the word action, to comprehend the forbearance too of any action proposed; sitting still, or holding one's peace, when walking or speaking are propos'd, though mere forbearances, requiring as much determination of the will, and being often as weighty in their consequences, as the contrary actions, may, on that consideration, well enough pass for actions too.[11]

8. *Essay,* book 2, chap. 21, sec. 16.
9. *Essay,* book 2, chap. 21, sec. 23 (1st ed.).
10. *Essay,* book 2, chap. 21, sec. 25.
11. *Essay,* book 2, chap. 21, sec. 28.

But if we do count refraining from doing A as itself an action, then his argument will also show that we are not free with respect to *acting*, for whenever an action is proposed to us we must either do that action or do the action that consists in forbearing the proposed action. Second, we need to distinguish between *not willing to do A* and *willing to refrain from doing A*. Suppose it is true that our agent must either will to do A or will to refrain from doing A—in short, that our agent is not free to avoid willing *anything*. It still may be true that our agent is free to avoid willing to do A. For what is it to be free with respect to willing a particular action? Clearly, it is to be free to determine whether one wills to do A or does not will to do A. And the fact, if it is a fact, that when doing A is proposed to us we must either will to do A or will to refrain from doing A does nothing to show that we are not free to will or not will doing A—nor does it show that we are not free to will or not will refraining from doing A. So Locke's first response to the question of whether a person is free to will is at best contrived and at worse utterly ineffective in establishing a negative answer to the question, once the question is properly posed in terms of whether a person is free to will to do A or not to will to do A.

Once freedom (liberty) is characterized as a power to act (or refrain from acting) *given* a prior willing so to act (or a prior willing to refrain from acting), it is not surprising that absurdity and regresses emerge when this notion of liberty is applied to acts of will and to the will itself. The real question concerning liberty of the will is whether, given the causes and circumstances in which he finds himself, a person, nevertheless, has a power to will to do an action and a power *not* to will to do that action. Locke isn't concerned to pose this question since he thinks that the act of will is *determined* by the causes and circumstances in which a person finds himself. His view in the first edition of the *Essay* is that willing is simply the mind preferring something—the willing to do A is simply the mind preferring to do A over refraining from doing A, and the willing to refrain from doing A is simply the mind preferring to refrain from doing A to doing A. Moreover, the will or preference of the mind is always determined by something outside of itself.[12] Thus, so far as the will is concerned, Locke appears to be close to Collins's view that a person is a necessary agent. Given the causes and circumstances a person is in, her will is determined in such a way that the act of will that occurs had to occur. If the person wills to perform a certain action, the causes and circumstances that determine that act of will are such that, given them, her willing to refrain from that action is not possible.

Earlier I remarked that although Hobbes and Collins certainly were necessitarians, it is only likely that Locke was. The reason for hesitating about Locke's commitment to necessitarianism is that in the second edition of the *Essay* he introduced a change that *may* be a concession to those who maintain that we must be free with respect to our willings if we are to be significantly free at all. As we've seen, the Locke of the first edition views our volitions as being necessitated by our desires, judgments, and circumstances. The strongest apparent good (first edition) or the strongest desire, that is, uneasiness (second edition), causally necessitates our act of will. But in the second edition Locke introduces what may be a concession to those who clamored for some degree of freedom of the will over against the determining force of the strongest desire.

> There being in us a great many uneasinesses always solliciting, and ready to determine the will, it is natural, as I have said, that the greatest, and most pressing should determine the will to the next action; and so it does for the most part, but not always. For the mind having in most cases, as is evident in experience, a power to suspend the execution and satisfaction of any of its desires, and so all, one after another, is at liberty to consider the

12. *Essay*, book 2, chap. 21, sec. 29 (1st ed.).

> objects of them; examine them on all sides, and weigh them with others. In this lies the liberty man has; and from the not using of it right comes all that variety of mistakes, errors, and faults which we run into, in the conduct of our lives, and our endeavours after happiness; whilst we precipitate the determination of our wills, and engage too soon before due examination. To prevent this we have a power to suspend the prosecution of this or that desire, as every one daily may experiment in himself. This seems to me the source of all liberty; in this seems to consist that, which is (as I think improperly) call'd free will. For during this suspension of any desire, before the will be determined to action, and the action (which follows that determination) done, we have opportunity to examine, view, and judge, of the good or evil of what we are going to do, and when, upon due examination, we have judg'd, we have done our duty, all that we can, or ought to do, in pursuit of our happiness; and 'tis not a fault, but a perfection of our nature to desire, will, and act according to the last result of a fair examination.[13]

The question that Locke leaves unanswered is what determines the will on a given occasion to suspend some desire that is otherwise strong enough to move the will toward some action. We can give an interpretation of this passage that is consistent with Locke's general account of freedom, an account that restricts freedom to the actions that flow from our acts of will. On this account we should construe a given instance of *suspending the execution of a desire* (the desire's bringing about a volition that is itself to begin an action to obtain the object of the desire) as itself an *action* that is brought about by a volition. The power to suspend the execution of a desire is, therefore, nothing more than the power to perform a certain action, like walking. On Locke's theory, to say that walking is in our power, that we are free to walk (at liberty to walk) is basically to say that we *can* walk *if* we will to walk. Similarly, on this interpretation of the above passage, to say that we are

13. *Essay,* book 2, chap. 21, sec. 47.

free to suspend the execution of desire is basically to say that we *can* suspend the execution of desire *if* we will to suspend the execution of desire. Of course, whether we do so will is not something that is in our power; it is not something we are free to do. If the volition to suspend does occur in us, it will have been necessitated by some second-order desire to have our first-order desires held in check until "we have opportunity to examine, view, and judge, of the good or evil of what we are going to do." But, as we have seen, on Locke's view this determination of the will does not abridge our freedom with respect to the action of suspending the execution of any first-order desire. For we can suspend or not suspend according as we will.

On the other hand, it is noteworthy that Locke does not tell us what, if anything, determines us to will the suspension of the execution of a desire, when we do so will. It could be that he meant to concede something to those who insist that our wills must enjoy a degree of freedom from the force of our desires. If so, then something like the following would be the proper interpretation of this passage: When the strongest desire is also found on reflection to be best to act on, we have no power to prevent the desire from immediately determining the will to action in pursuit of the object of the desire. However, we normally do have power effectively to will the suspension of the execution of the strongest desire until we have had an opportunity to determine whether it is best on the whole to act on that desire. Moreover, this power over the willing to suspend is an original power of the person. The person may exercise that power or not; and no desires determine the person to will (or not will) suspending the execution of a first-order desire. Of course, some first-order desire may reach a degree of intensity that overcomes the power to suspend its execution. But when this is not the case, there is a freedom with respect to willing or not willing the suspension of the execution of that desire.

Between these two interpretations there may be others

more or less palatable to necessitarians and the advocates of free will. In any case, we must leave it to Locke scholars to determine whether he intended this important addition to the second edition as a concession to the advocates of free will. It is worth noting, however, that Collins does so interpret the passage. Having earlier observed that Locke's account of freedom is perfectly consistent with our wills being totally determined by our desires, judgments, and circumstances, Collins refers to the passage from Locke quoted above and clearly understands it as extending liberty to the will itself, as opposed to actions resulting from our volition. "Hence appears the mistake of those who think me at liberty to will, or not to will, because, say they, they can suspend willing."[14] Collins goes on to argue that there is no reason to think that the act of will to suspend willing an action is any more free from causal necessity than is the willing of an action.

For our purposes, we will construe Lockean freedom as the account of freedom Locke presents in the first edition of the *Essay.* On this account freedom applies to actions that flow from our acts of will (volitions); freedom is inapplicable to the will itself and to the various determinations of the will (volitions). With this account before us, it is time now to consider what appear to be the most salient objections to it.

There are two major, traditional objections to Lockean freedom. Before considering these two traditional objections, however, we should consider an objection due to J. L. Austin, since it attacks a point that is assumed by the other objections. Locke and Collins, as we just saw, took the view that *given* the causes of your action A, you could not have done anything other than A. Yet this does not preclude it being true that you could have done something else *if* you had willed to do something else. For with a difference in the causes, we might expect a difference in our powers. Now this nice harmony of causal necessity and freedom of action presupposes that the

14. *Human Liberty,* 38.

'if' in statements of the form 'S could have done X if S had chosen or willed to do X' is an 'if' of causal condition. And Austin had an apparently devastating argument to show that the 'if' in 'S could have done X if S had chosen or willed to do X' is not the 'if' of causal condition.[15] The argument is this: If we consider an 'if' of causal condition, as in the statement, 'This zinc will dissolve if placed in that acid,' we can note two points. First, it will follow that if this zinc does not dissolve then it has not been placed in that acid. Second, it will not follow simpliciter that this zinc will dissolve. Just the opposite holds, however, of statements of the form 'S could have done X if S had chosen or willed to do X.' First it will *not* follow that if S could not have done X then S has not chosen or willed to do X. And second it *will* follow simpliciter that S could have done X. From these premises Austin concludes that the 'if' in 'S could have done X if S had chosen or willed to do X' is not the 'if' of causal condition. But all that really follows from these premises is that the 'if' in 'S could have done X if S had chosen or willed to do X' does not present a condition of the *main clause,* 'S could have done X.' It may still be, for all Austin has shown, an 'if' of causal condition of something else. What else? Clearly, as Kurt Baier has argued, it would have to be of S's doing X.[16] The 'if' in 'S could have done X if S had chosen or willed to do X' is an 'if' of causal condition of the doing of X by S. What statements of this form tell us is that a set of conditions necessary for S's doing X obtained at the time in question, and had S chosen or willed to do X there would then have been a set of conditions sufficient for S's doing X. On this account, 'S could have done X if S had chosen or willed to do X' implies the genuinely conditional statement form, 'S would have done X if S had chosen or

15. J. L. Austin, "Ifs and Cans," *Proceedings of the British Academy* 42 (1956): 107–32.

16. Kurt Baier, "Could and Would," *Analysis,* Supplement 13 (1963): 20–29.

willed to do X.' So Austin's argument fails to establish that Locke and Collins were wrong to suppose that the 'if' in 'S could have done X if S had chosen or willed to do X' is an 'if' of condition.

The first traditional objection begins by noting that Lockean freedom, as we saw, exists solely at the level of *action:* you are free provided you have the power to do the act if you will to do it, and have the power not to do it if you will not to do it. But what about the *will?* What if you don't have the power to will the action, or don't have the power not to will it? To see the difficulty here, let's return to our example where you are sitting down, someone asks you to get up and walk over to the window to see what is happening outside, but you are quite satisfied where you are and choose to remain sitting. We earlier supposed that I had injected you with a powerful drug so that you can't move your legs. Here Locke would say that you don't sit *freely* since it was not in your power to do otherwise if you had willed otherwise—say, to get up and walk to the window. But let's now suppose that instead of paralyzing your legs I had hooked up a machine to your brain so that I can and do deprive you of the *capacity* to will to do otherwise. It's still true that you have the power to get up and walk *if* you should will to do so—I haven't taken away your physical capacity to walk, as I did when I paralyzed your legs. Here the problem is that you have no power over your will. In this case, it seems clear that you sit of necessity, not freely. On Locke's account of freedom, however, it remains true that you sit freely and not of necessity. And this being so, we must conclude that Locke's account of freedom is simply inadequate. Freedom that is worth the name, therefore, must include power *to will or not will,* not simply power *to do if we will.*

There is a second, traditional objection to Lockean freedom, an objection based on the fact that Lockean freedom is consistent with the causal necessity of our actions and decisions. According to the necessitarians, you are totally determined to will and act as you do by your motives and circumstances. Indeed, Leibniz quotes with favor Bayle's comparison of the influence of motives on an agent to the influence of weights on a balance. Referring to Bayle, Leibniz remarks: "According to him, one can explain what passes in our resolutions by the hypothesis that the will of man is like a balance which is at rest when the weights of its two pans are equal, and which always inclines either to one side or the other according to which of the pans is the more heavily laden."[17] Bayle's idea is that just as the heavier weight determines the movement of the balance, so does the stronger motive determine the movement of your will. If your motive to get up and walk to the window is stronger than whatever motive you have to remain sitting, then it determines you to will to get up and walk to the window. Given the respective strength of these motives, it is no more possible for you to will to remain sitting than it is possible for a balance to stay even when a heavier weight is placed in one of its pans than in the other. Motives, on this view, are determining causes of the decisions of our will in precisely the way in which weights are the determining causes of the movements of the balance. But if all this is so, claim the opponents of the necessitarians, then no one acts freely, no one has power over his will. For it is generally agreed that our motives are determined by factors largely beyond our control, and if these motives determine our acts of will as weights determine the movement of a balance, then we can no more control our will than the balance can control its movements. Just as a balance has no freedom of movement, so the person would have no freedom of will. Freedom would be an illusion if our will is subject to causal necessity by motives and circumstances. Since Lockean freedom is consistent with such causal necessity, Lockean freedom is really not freedom at all.[18]

We've looked at two major, traditional objections to Lock-

17. *Theodicy,* III. para. 324.

18. These two objections, and others, are expressed by Reid, Clarke, and Edmund Law. Perhaps their most forceful presentation is contained in Clarke's stinging attack on Collins's work. See *Remarks upon a Book, Entitled, A Philosophical Enquiry Concerning Human Liberty* in Samuel Clarke, *The Works,* vol. 4.

ean freedom. According to Locke, freedom to do a certain thing is (roughly) the power to do that thing if we will to do it. Our first objection is that we might have the power to do something if we willed to do it, and yet lack the power over our will. Surely, freedom must include the power to will or not will, and not just the power to do *if* we will. Our second objection is against the necessitarian view that our acts of will are causally necessitated by prior events and circumstances over which we have little or no control. If that is so then we have no more control over what we will to do than a balance has over how it moves once the weights are placed in its pans. Causal necessitation of our acts of will denies to us any real power over the determinations of our will. And without such power we do not act freely. To be told, as Locke would tell us, that we could have done something else if we had so willed, is of course interesting and perhaps not unimportant. But if we are totally determined to will as we do and cannot will otherwise, then it is absurd to say we act freely simply because had we willed otherwise—which we could not do—we could have acted otherwise.

I believe these objections reveal serious inadequacies in Locke's conception of freedom. Indeed, it puzzles me that the notion of Lockean freedom continues to survive in the face of such weighty objections. But before passing on to consider the position of the advocates of free will (the libertarians) we should note an attempt or two to defend or amend Lockean freedom so that it will appear less implausible.

At the level of action we are free for Locke provided we could have done otherwise if we had chosen or willed to do otherwise. Basically, our objections to Lockean freedom point out the need to supplement freedom at the level of action with freedom at the level of the will. The problem is how to do this without abandoning the causal necessitation of the act of will by our motives and circumstances. Now one might be tempted to suggest that at the level of the will we are free provided we could have willed to do otherwise *if* we had been in different circumstances or had different motives—a thesis that in no way conflicts with the act of will being causally necessitated by our actual motives and circumstances. Such a suggestion of what it means to have free will fully merits, I believe, the contempt and ridicule that Kant meant when he spoke of a "wretched subterfuge" and James meant when he spoke of "a quagmire of evasion."[19] If Lockean freedom is to be saved, we need a better account of free will than this suggestion provides.

In his discussion of Locke's account of freedom, Leibniz generally endorses Locke's view but points out its failure to provide any account of free will. He suggests two accounts of free will, one in contrast to the bondage of the passions, an account drawn from the Stoics; a second in contrast to necessity, an account that is Leibniz's own. Concerning the first, he remarks: "the Stoics said that only the wise man is free; and one's mind is indeed not free when it is possessed by a great passion, for then one cannot will as one should, i.e. with proper deliberation. It is in that way that God alone is perfectly free, and that created minds are free only in proportion as they are above passion."[20] Here we have a nice supplementation of Lockean freedom. For an action to be free it must not only be willed and such that we could have done otherwise if we had willed otherwise, but also the act of will must have been free in the sense of resulting at least partially from the exercise of reason. If the passions of a madman totally determine his act of will and the consequent action, we need not say that he acts freely. However, if the judgments of reason and our circumstances totally determine our will so that given those judgments and circumstances no other act of will was possible, we can still say that we act freely provided we could

19. See Kant's *Critique of Practical Reason,* 99. Also see William James's "The Dilemma of Determinism" in *The Writings of William James,* ed. John J. McDermott (Chicago: University of Chicago Press, 1977), 590.

20. *New Essays on Human Understanding,* 175.

have done otherwise had we chosen or willed to do otherwise, for as rational beings we are willing as we should. This amendment, I believe, softens the necessitarian view; but it fails to solve the basic problem. For to will as we should is one thing, and to will freely is another. The problem with Lockean freedom is not that it fails to rule out necessitation of the will *by the passions;* the problem is that it fails to rule out the necessitation of the will *period.*

In his second account of free will Leibniz insists that the act of will must be free in the sense of not being necessitated by the motives and circumstances that give rise to it. His often repeated doctrine on this matter is that motives "incline without necessitating." This doctrine has the appearance of giving the free will advocate just what he wants, the power to have willed otherwise even though the motives and circumstances be unchanged. But Leibniz meant no such thing. The motive that inclines most determines the will and the action, just as the weight that is heaviest determines the movement of the balance. Motives and circumstances necessitate the act of will in the sense that it is logically or causally impossible that those motives and circumstances should obtain and the act of will not obtain. Leibniz's claim that they don't necessitate the act of will means only that the act of will *itself* is not thereby something that is an absolute or logical necessity.[21] I conclude that although the first account Leibniz gives of free will, the account he traces to the Stoics, does provide an amendment to Lockean freedom that makes it less implausible, Leibniz's famous dictum that motives incline without necessitating provides no help at all.[22] It is time to turn to the central thesis of the advocates of free will.

21. For a more extended account of this interpretation of Leibniz's dictum, "motives incline but do not necessitate," see G. H. R. Parkinson, *Leibniz on Human Freedom* (Wiesbaden: Franz Steiner Verlag, 1970), 50–53.

22. This remark assumes that the proper interpretation of Leibniz's dictum is the one I offer, the one developed at greater length by G. H. R. Parkinson (see previous note).

2

Background: Clarke's Conception of Agency

> For whatever acts necessarily, does not indeed act at all, but is only acted upon; is not at all an agent, but a mere patient; does not move, but is moved only.
>
> —Samuel Clarke

Locke holds that once a prisoner's chains are knocked off and the prison door set open to him, he is "perfectly at liberty, because he may either go or stay as he best likes." And this perfect liberty, Locke contends, is in no way abridged by the fact that the prisoner's fear of the darkness of the night *makes* him choose to stay in his prison.

Although Clarke seldom mentions Locke, his own statement of liberty may have been written with Locke's conception of freedom in mind.

> For the essence of liberty . . . consists in his being an agent, that is, in his having a continual power of choosing, whether he shall act, or whether he shall forbear acting. Which power of agency or free choice . . . is not at all prevented by chains or prisons: for a man who chooses to indeavour to move out of his place, is therein as much a free agent, as he that actually moves out of his place.[1]

1. Samuel Clarke, *Discourse Concerning the Being and Attributes of God,* 101.

According to Clarke, the essence of freedom consists in *being an agent,* and to be an agent is to have power over one's will, to have a continual power of willing an action or not willing the action. Moreover, as Clarke sees it, the possession of such a power is in no way abridged by restraints that prevent one from successfully completing the action willed. The chains take away the power to leave; they do not take away the power to will to leave. (Of course, one who knows he is in chains may see the pointlessness of choosing to leave and, therefore, not exercise his power so to choose.)

Let us call those who believe that we have, or sometimes have, a power to will or not will various actions *libertarians.* As we proceed, it will become increasingly clear that the defining mark of libertarianism, the assertion that we have, or sometimes have, a power to will or not will, is to be so understood that we cannot possess such power if our acts of will are causally necessitated by prior events and circumstances. Therefore, *necessitarianism,* the claim that we have Lockean freedom (or some variation on Lockean freedom) and that our acts of will are causally necessitated by our motives, judgments, and circumstances is incompatible with *libertarianism.*[2] The libertarian does not contest the thesis that Lockean freedom is consistent with our volitions being causally necessitated by prior desires, judgments, and circumstances. Nor does the necessitarian contest the thesis that the sort of freedom espoused by Clarke and Reid is inconsistent with our volitions being causally necessitated by prior events and circumstances. The issue between them is which conception of

2. The key idea in necessitarianism is the causal necessitation of our acts of will by earlier events and circumstances. One could accept this idea, acknowledge that Lockean freedom is compatible with it, and yet agree with the libertarians that Lockean freedom is a wholly inadequate conception of freedom. Such a view is not under study in this essay. Since it is not, I use the term 'necessitarianism' in a more restricted sense to stand for the key idea and the claim that some version of Lockean freedom is an adequate conception of freedom.

freedom is more adequate to our common-sense beliefs about freedom and moral responsibility and more adequate to our general metaphysical and scientific principles. Although our attention in this study will be focused primarily on the libertarian conception of freedom, particularly as developed and defended by Reid, it is impossible not to enter into some general discussion of the arguments for and against both conceptions of freedom—the freedom of action favored by Locke and Collins and the freedom of the will favored by Clarke and Reid. In the next chapter we will consider the chief arguments Collins advances against libertarianism. Here we will enlarge our understanding of Clarke's conception of agency, a conception that plays a central role in the libertarian account of freedom.

As we have noted, in 1717 Collins took up the cause of the necessitarians in his popular *A Philosophical Inquiry Concerning Human Liberty.* Whether confused or just to be daring and perhaps mischievous, Collins at one point cited Clarke as espousing the necessitarian cause.[3] This proved to be a mistake. Clarke responded with a devastating attack, an attack that left many of Collins's points and arguments in disarray. Indeed, Clarke's short response is a brilliant embodiment of the polemical essay, an art form that reached its zenith in the eighteenth century. It is the mark of this form of writing to charge first that the idea under attack is an absolute self-contradiction; second, that it leads to atheism; and third, that it destroys all morality. When these points have been conclusively demonstrated, the author of the idea under attack is then noted to be ignorant and to have a questionable character.

Among the ideas attacked by Clarke was Collins's central proposal: that "man is a *necessary agent.*" Clarke argues that the very idea of a necessary agent is a *self-contradictory* idea. "For whatever acts necessarily, does not indeed act at all, but is only acted upon; is not at all an agent, but a mere patient;

3. See Collins's *Human Liberty,* 112; also see Clarke's *Works,* 4:725.

does not move, but is moved only."[4] His point seems to be this: If all the "actions" ascribed to a person are the result of a series of necessary causes, then they are changes that occur in the person; she is *passive* with respect to these changes; she undergoes these changes and does not produce them. But if the person is the *agent* of her "actions" then the person is not passive with respect to them; she is the active cause of these changes, not simply an object in which these changes are caused to occur by other things or changes.

As a first effort in responding to this important argument, we can distinguish between changes in the person that are due to the person's motives, desires, and the like and changes in the person that are due to physical processes without or within the person over which she has little or no control.[5] Changes of the latter sort—pulsations of the heart, convulsive jerkings of one's limbs, etc.—are changes which the person undergoes and does not actively produce. It is among changes of the former sort that we locate "actions." These "actions" are held to be produced by the person as agent, even though (or just because?) they are the causal effects of the person's reasons, motives, and the like.

The point to be drawn from the distinction between two different sorts of causes is this: The mere fact that some change in a person has a necessary cause does not rule out the person as the active cause or agent of that change and thus does not preclude that change from being an action. If the necessary cause of the change is a physical process over which the person has no control, then the person is not the agent of the change but is a mere patient—she undergoes the change and the change is not an action. But if the necessary cause of the change is the person's own desires and reasons, then the

4. *Works*, 4:722.

5. In saying that motives, desires, and so on are the causes of these changes ("actions"), I don't mean that they are the immediate causes. For Locke and Collins, the reasons, motives, etc. cause certain *volitions* in the person which then cause the motions or changes which are held to be actions.

person may be the agent of the change, the active cause of the change, and that change may be an action.

Undoubtedly, this way of rescuing the idea of a necessary agent from the charge of inconsistency would be lost on Clarke. For Clarke holds that "to be an agent, signifies, to have a power of beginning motion."[6] But if the changes in the person have necessary causes in earlier things or changes, then the person has no power to *initiate* these changes (motions). There is no *beginning of motion* in the person at the time of (or just prior to) the "actions"; there is at best only a change in the person wrought by earlier things and changes. If we make reasons and motives *necessary causes* of those changes in the person which we call "actions," then, although it may be interesting to note that reasons and motives aren't mere physical processes, we still make the person a mere *patient* with regard to those changes and not an *agent*—for there is then no "beginning of motion" (change) brought about by the person at the time of, or just prior to, the "actions."

Clarke's contention that an agent has *active* power, the power to *begin* motion, is not introduced into the debate with Collins's "out of the blue." Similar notions were current in Locke's discussion of the ideas of active and passive power. These two ideas are meant to mark the obvious difference between something that has a power to bring about a change in something else (active power) and something that has a power to be changed by something else (passive power). When one billiard ball strikes another it "produces" a change in the second ball, putting it in motion. The second ball has a passive power to be put in motion by the "active power" of the first ball striking it. But if the first ball was set in motion by a billiard stick, does it (the first ball) really exert *active power* when setting in motion the second ball upon striking it? Locke thinks this example gives us only "a very obscure idea of an *active* power of moving in body, whilst we observe it only to

6. *Works,* 4:722.

transfer, but not *produce* any motion. For it is but a very obscure idea of power which reaches not the production of the action, but the continuation of the passion."[7] The idea of active power, Locke argues, is the power of *beginning motion,* an idea we get best from reflection on ourselves and not from observations of the "actions" of bodies on one another. "So that it seems to me, we have from the observation of the operation of bodies by our senses, but a very imperfect obscure idea of *active* power; since they afford us not an idea in themselves of the power to begin any action, either motion or thought."[8]

When we reflect upon ourselves we find, Locke says, "a *power* to begin or forbear, continue or end several actions of our minds, and motions of our bodies. . . . This *power* which the mind has . . . to prefer the motion of any part of the body to its rest, and *vice versa,* in any particular instance, is that which we call *will.*"[9] What is remarkable about this passage is that there is nothing in its characterization of the will with which Clarke would disagree. In fact, it says just what Clarke *means* by agency and freedom of will. In the passage quoted earlier from Clarke, he is obviously thinking of actions that involve motions of the body. The person is an agent and free just in case he has the power to begin a motion and the power to forbear beginning a motion in the body. (The exercise of this power to begin a motion or forbear beginning a motion is a *volition.*) Clarke's complaint against Collins is that if the person is determined by prior things or events (reasons, motives, etc.) to will a certain motion in the body, then the person is not really an agent, for her power of bringing about a motion in the body is a passive power like the power of the first billiard ball, having been set in motion, to transfer motion to the second ball upon striking against it.

7. *Essay,* book 2, chap. 21, sec. 4.
8. *Essay,* book 2, chap. 21, sec. 4.
9. *Essay,* book 2, chap. 21, sec. 5.

Our problem is this. Both Locke and Clarke view the agent as possessing *active power,* power to begin a motion and power to forbear beginning a motion. Clarke thinks that to have such a power is to be a free agent. Locke, however, holds that any act of will is causally determined by prior events and circumstances, something which, if true, means for Clarke that we are not free agents at all, that we really have no active power, no power to begin a motion or to forbear beginning a motion. Clearly, then, either Clarke and Locke mean something different by the power to begin (forbear) a motion, or one of them (at least) is simply wrong—Clarke in thinking that such a power is inconsistent with the causal determination of our acts of will, or Locke in thinking that such a power is consistent with the causal determination of our acts of will.

My suggestion is that Locke and Clarke really have different understandings of the nature of active power. Clarke takes active power to be *unconditional.* If a person has the power to begin motion, this does not mean that he has this power on the condition that some prior event did, or did not, occur. Locke, however, as we have already seen from his discussion of the power to do (refrain from doing) some action, presents a *conditional account* of power. Thus, for Locke, one has the power to raise his arm provided he *can* raise his arm *if* he so wills. Extending this account to the will, Locke's view, I suggest, is that one has the power to will to raise his arm (begin a certain motion) provided he *can* will to raise his arm *if* doing so would be what he judges best. On this view, Locke can allow that the person's judgment that it is best to raise his arm causally necessitates his willing to raise it, and yet maintain that he has the power to will to forbear raising his arm (forbear beginning a certain motion). For on the conditional account of power favored by Locke, one has that power provided that he can will to refrain from raising his arm if he judges that doing so would be best. Thus, on Locke's view, the causal necessitation of an act of will by the judgment of the understanding concerning what is best to be done does not abridge the agent's power to will otherwise.[10]

On Clarke's unconditional account, however, it is clear that given the causal necessitation of some act of will by some prior event or state (a judgment, say, that the course of action willed is the best), the person no longer has the power to forbear willing. For the person no longer has any power over the occurrence of the judgment that the course of action willed is the best, and given that judgment we are supposing that nothing else can happen other than the act of will that the judgment produces. Moreover, it won't do even to say that the agent has the power to bring about the act of will that is causally necessitated, losing only the power to forbear so willing. For Clarke insists, as will Reid, that power to do implies power not to do. "All power of acting, essentially implies at the same time a power of not acting: otherwise it is not acting, but barely a being acted upon by that power (whatever it be) which causes the action."[11]

Given what we've just concluded, what can we say in response to Clarke's argument that since being an agent signifies a power to begin (forbear beginning) a motion, the idea of a necessary agent is contradictory? Our first effort to respond to this argument by distinguishing between what were called *moral* causes (reasons, motives, and the like) and *physical* causes of movements of the body is not sufficient. For on Clarke's view, *any* backward series of determining causes (a series that has members preceding and necessitating the person's *volitions*) renders the person a patient and not an agent with respect to those bodily motions. The person cannot be an

10. The essential problem with Locke's view (if this was his view) is that on the necessitarian account our volitions are ultimately necessitated by events beyond our control. This being so, it is scant comfort to be assured that we could have willed otherwise had some earlier event (that did not occur) occurred. It is for this reason that I earlier (in Chapter 1) treated this account of power over the will with some degree of scorn.

11. *Works,* 4:722.

agent with respect to those movements, for the person cannot be said to *begin* those motions or changes.

Clearly, the issue, at least in part, now becomes what is *meant* by the person *beginning* the bodily motion. On Clarke's view, to begin a motion is to cause that motion but not to be caused to cause that motion. But there is no reason thus far given why Locke and Collins must accept this view. Why not say that the person begins the bodily motion just in case the person *wills* that motion and the motion results from that act of will? If the bodily motion (say, the arm's rising) is not caused by the person's willing to raise the arm, instead being caused by physical processes over which the person has no control, then the bodily motion is not *begun* by the person. Bodily motions (an arm's rising and the like) are *begun* by the person just in case the person wills the bodily motion (perhaps we should also say that the willing, given the circumstances, causes the bodily motion, the arm's rising, in an appropriate way). In any case, there is a clear difference to be drawn between whether the arm's rising results from the person's willing it or results from physical processes that are independent of such an act of will. Why not mark this difference by saying that in the former case the person *begins* the bodily motion (and thus is the *agent* of an action) and in the latter case the bodily motion is a change (not an action) with respect to which the person is a patient and not an agent? If Clarke insists that only his contra-causal account explicates what is *meant* by a person *beginning* a motion, isn't it reasonable to retort that his account *begs the question* against the idea of a necessary agent? Or, to be more precise, shouldn't we distinguish two ideas of agency? On one idea a person is an agent with respect to a bodily change just in case the bodily change results from her willing it (regardless of whether her willing that change has a determining cause). On the second idea (Clarke's) a person is an *agent* with respect to a bodily change just in case the bodily change results from her willing it and there is no determining cause that brings it about that she wills that change. On the second idea of what it is to be an agent, Clarke is indeed right in claiming that Collins's idea of a necessary agent is a contradictory idea. But on the first idea of what it is to be an agent there is no contradiction in Collins's thesis that we are necessary agents. Clarke is, of course, free to attach whatever meaning he likes to the idea of being an agent. But it is another matter when he claims that *Collins's* thesis that man is a necessary agent is contradictory. For Collins's idea of what it is to be an agent with respect to bodily motion, what it is to have active power with respect to bodily motion, is clearly no more than to have the power to begin (refrain from beginning) a bodily motion *according as the understanding directs.* I conclude, therefore, that Clarke's argument that Collins's idea of a necessary agent is contradictory begs the question against the Locke-Collins position. This is not to say that Clarke's argument is defective in the sense of being invalid or lacking true premises. It is simply to say that it is ineffective as a piece of reasoning against anyone who is sympathetic to the view that persons are agents and do have active power, even though their actions are traceable causally to volitions of the person that themselves have determining causes in prior states of the person.

3

Background: Collins's Arguments against Libertarianism

Liberty therefore, or a power to act or not to act, to do this or another thing under the same causes, is an *impossibility* and *atheistical.*

—Anthony Collins

In his treatise *Human Liberty,* Collins presents several arguments in favor of necessitarianism and against libertarianism. He argues (1) that human experience provides no rational proof of free will, (2) that libertarianism is inconsistent with basic principles of causality, (3) that free will would be an imperfection in us and harmful to morality, (4) that free will is inconsistent with divine foreknowledge, and (5) that if persons were not determined in their actions and willing, rewards and punishments would make no sense. Some of these arguments will be taken up later. Here it will be profitable to look with some care at his arguments to show that the principles of causality are inconsistent with libertarianism. My belief is that such an examination, both of Collins's arguments and Clarke's replies, will enable us to see more deeply into the assumptions underlying the libertarian position, assumptions concerning causality and agency. Such an examination will also set the stage for our study of the libertarian position as worked out in some detail by its most capable advocate, Thomas Reid.

Having satisfied himself that experience is on the side of

necessity, Collins appeals to certain principles concerning causality, principles that he thinks clearly establish that the human person is a necessary agent, that libertarianism is an illusion. (A necessary agent, on Collins's view, is a person whose actions and volitions are causally necessitated by earlier events.)

> A second reason to prove man a necessary agent is, because all his actions have a beginning. For whatever has a beginning must have a cause; and every cause is a necessary cause.[1]

From his subsequent discussion, it is clear that Collins sees two distinct principles at work in this argument.

I. Whatever has a beginning has a cause.
II. Every cause is a necessary cause.

Because so many have taken the view that the free will position holds that acts of will are *uncaused,* I propose to break up Collins's "second reason" into two distinct arguments. The first argument relies only on principle I and may be expressed as follows:

1. If we have free will then there are volitions that are uncaused.
2. Volitions have a beginning.
3. Whatever has a beginning has a cause.

therefore,
We do not have free will.

Clarke and other exponents of rationalistic theology all

1. *Human Liberty,* 57.

held principle I as a fundamental principle of reason.[2] Indeed, in opposition to Locke, Clarke, but not Reid, held with Leibniz a much stronger principle. Principle I does not require that there be a determining reason or cause of an eternal being, a being that never came into existence. The stronger principle—whatever exists has a cause (or determining reason)—was essential to Clarke's celebrated "demonstration" of the existence of God. So Clarke, as well as the other advocates of free will, certainly embraced principle I. What they denied in this argument was premise 1. Although they held that free will precluded the will being *caused* by motives, desires, and the like, they did not hold that acts of will (volitions) are uncaused. The prevailing view held by the advocates of free will is that those thoughts and bodily motions that are *actions* are caused by volitions, and the volitions themselves, although not caused by any other events, are *caused* by the *person* whose volitions they are. It is true that Clarke and others vacillate in their descriptions of what it is that causes volitions. Clarke himself sometimes says it is the person, sometimes the soul, and sometimes the principle or power of self-motion that is in the soul. But no advocate of the libertarian position held that volitions and/or actions are uncaused. The most frequently stated view is that the person, by virtue of having a self-moving principle or power, is the cause of the volition to perform a certain action.

The mistaken idea that the advocates of the free will hold

2. Two senses of 'cause' need to be distinguished. In the primary sense, according to the libertarians, a cause is always an *agent* who has power to bring about some change (the effect) in himself or in some other thing. In a secondary sense, a cause is some prior event or state that is related by a law of nature to a change (the effect). The advocates of free will embraced principle I, using 'cause' in the primary sense. The opponents of free will embraced principle I but tended to use 'cause' in the secondary sense. Considerable confusion in the debate over liberty and necessity is due, I believe, to a failure to recognize which sense of 'cause' is being used by a writer in presenting his case for or against free will.

volitions and/or actions to be uncaused is likely due to the fact that the advocates deny the sorts of causes affirmed by the necessitarians: motives, desires, reasons, and the like. Thus, referring to Leibniz and Collins, Edmund Law, a libertarian, remarks:

> Lastly, to the Argument against the *Possibility* of such a Liberty, so frequently repeated by the two Authors above mentioned, viz. that Actions done without any Motive, would be *Effects* without a *Cause;* we reply, in short, that it is a plain *Petitio Principii,* in supposing Motives to be the real *physical efficient* Causes . . . of Volition or Action, which we deny; and yet are far from supposing these Acts to be absolutely without a Cause; nay we assign them another, and affirm that their only true and proper Cause is this self-moving Power, and the only Cause of this is the Creator who communicated it.[3]

Of course, once it is pointed out that the agent himself is the cause of his volition, the necessitarian will want to know what *change* in the agent causes his volition. For the necessitarian also holds that the agent causes his volition—but he explains this by saying that some change in the agent (his coming to have certain motives, his making certain judgments, etc.) causes the agent to have the volition in question. And at this point we come to a serious parting of the ways between the necessitarians and the libertarians. Both allow that the agent causes his volition. The necessitarians understand this in terms of some *event* involving the agent causing his volition; whereas the free will advocates view the *agent himself* as the cause in virtue of his self-moving power.[4] In the one case we have one event in the agent (his judging that a certain course of action is best) causing another event in the

3. See William King, *Essay on the Origin of Evil,* 354.

4. For stylistic variation I will sometimes use the expression 'free will advocates' in place of the expression 'libertarians.'

agent (his volition); whereas in the other case we have a substance (the person) causing an event (his volition).

Perhaps we can get at the heart of the free will position if we ask and try to answer two questions. Our first question is this: *What does the agent do to bring about his volition?* Often when we do something, we do something else in order to do it. For example, in order to write a letter we grasp a pen and move the muscles in our arm and hand. If then, as the free will advocate claims, the person brings about his volition, what does he do to bring it about? The free will advocate says that the person (or the soul of the person) brings about his volition by virtue of a self-determining power. Fair enough. But doesn't the person (soul) exert itself or exercise its power in some way in order to bring about this effect, the volition? Once this is admitted, however, we have explained the occurrence of one event, the volition, not simply by reference to a substance (the person or soul) and a power to determine the will, but by reference to another event, the act of exertion by the soul.[5] And what then causes this act of exertion? Perhaps the person's judging that it is best now to write a letter causes the exertion which results in the volition to write a letter. But, as Clarke himself admits, judgments are necessitated by prior causes, etc.[6] So if the libertarian allows that some act of exertion by the person brings about his volition, he appears to take an important step down the slippery slope that ends with his volition being causally necessitated and, therefore, with free will being abridged.

Some necessitarians take the view that the only way in

5. This problem is discussed at length in Chapter 8 with respect to Reid's theory of freedom.

6. Clarke distinguishes perceiving and judging from willing and acting. Following Locke, he holds that the person is largely, if not entirely, passive with respect to perceiving and judging. Attending, he allows, is often an action. But if I do look at the sun I have no power to see other than what I see; similarly, for judgments of the understanding concerning truth or falsehood, as well as our assent to propositions judged true. In all these respects the agent is passive, or largely so.

which the person (or soul) can bring about a volition is by engaging in some act of exertion that is distinct from the volition which is the causal effect. Thus, Jonathan Edwards remarks:

> to say the faculty, or the soul determines its own volition, but not by any act, is a contradiction. Because for the soul to *direct, decide* or *determine* anything, is to act; and this is supposed; for the soul is here spoken of as being a cause in this affair, bringing something to pass, or doing something; or, which is the same thing, exerting itself in order to an effect, which effect is the determination of volition, or the particular kind and manner of an act of will. But certainly, this exertion or action is not the same with the effect, in order to the production of which it is exerted, but must be something prior to it.[7]

Clearly, the free will advocate who holds that the person is the cause of her volition cannot take the view that whenever a person causes some event, there is some other event that she first causes in order to bring about the event in question. Consistent with his basic position that there is such a thing as *substance causation* that is not reducible to *causation by events,* the free will advocate must hold that *some event* that causally results in an action must have as its *immediate cause* the agent herself, and not some earlier event such as an act of exertion.[8] And a rather plausible candidate for this position is the *volition* that gives rise to the action.[9] When an agent brings about (causes) his volition, therefore, there is not some event (an act

7. *Freedom of Will,* 175–76.

8. A different position on this issue is developed with respect to Reid's theory in Chapter 8.

9. This appears to be Clarke's view. Clarke notes that 'willing' is ambiguous, sometimes signifying 'the last perception of the understanding,' and sometimes signifying 'the first exertion of the self-moving or active faculty.' *Works* 4:727. Since he holds that the former generally does not fall within our power, Clarke clearly favors the second signification. As we shall see, Reid distinguishes the exertion from the volition.

of exertion) he brings about which is the immediate cause of the volition. (I'm here describing what I take to be the logical implications of Clarke's view.) The immediate cause of the volition is the agent, the person whose volition it is. To the question, What does the agent do to bring about his volition?, the proper answer of the free will advocate is "Nothing!" The agent wills something. His act of will is the volition. But the agent does not *do something* that produces his act of will.[10] To hold, as Edwards does, that such a view is contradictory is to beg the question against the view that a substance may be the immediate cause of an event by virtue of possessing the power to determine the will. The person has the power to determine the will, and the *act* of the person by which the will is determined *is* simply the occurrence of the volition.

If we allow that the agent as substance, and not some *act* of the agent, may be the immediate cause of the volition, there is a second question we need to raise. *What is it that causes the agent to bring about her volition?* The importance of this question is twofold. First, it reveals that the necessitarian position need not be tied to the denial of irreducible substance causation. Someone who, like Collins, believes in a chain of causes determining volition and action can allow that the person as substance (rather than some event) is the immediate cause of her volition and still hold that the volition is causally determined by prior states and events. For he may argue that the agent's judgments, desires, etc., causally determine the agent to substance-cause her volition.[11] That is, instead of saying that the volition is the immediate causal product of the desires, etc., he may say that the agent herself causes the volition but is herself causally determined by desires, motives, and the like to thus cause her volition. Second, since the free

10. A somewhat different view of this matter is held by Reid. We will discuss his view of this matter in Chapters 4, 5, and 8.

11. As we will see in Chapter 4, on Reid's view of agent causation, it is *not possible* to cause an agent to agent-cause some effect.

will advocate must deny that prior states or events causally determine the agent to cause her volition (when free will is operative), the necessitarian can reintroduce his charge that the free will position is in violation of the principle that whatever has a beginning has a cause. For although, given the idea of irreducible substance-causation, the free will advocate can provide a cause for the agent's volition, he seems to be unable to assign a cause of the agent's causing her volition. But if the-agent's-causing-her-volition falls under the expression "has a beginning," we have a violation of principle I. Having seen the importance of this second question, we must now see what the libertarian can say in response to it.

There are, I believe, only two lines of response open to the free will advocate. The first line is to deny that *the-agent's-causing-her-volition* falls under the expression "has a beginning." The volition itself is datable in time and thus has a beginning. (There was a time at which the volition was not occurring, and a later time at which it occurred.) As such, the volition must, given principle I, have a cause. But when we look carefully at the-agent's-causing-her-volition, we might argue that it is not an event at all, and does not have a beginning. The human agent herself, of course, has a beginning. The volition itself also has a beginning. But there is no third thing or event, the-agent's-causing-her-volition, that has a beginning.[12] Following this line, the free will advocate may ar-

12. Taking the phrase 'has a beginning' literally, it is false that the agent's-causing-her-volition has no beginning. At the very least, there was a time before which the agent was not causing her volition and a time after which the agent was no longer causing her volition. In claiming that whatever has a beginning has a cause, however, what was being held is (1) that every substance that *begins to exist* has a cause and (2) that every *change* that a substance undergoes has a cause. If I will to move my arm, then I undergo a change; a volition occurs in me that was not occurring prior to my act of will to move my arm. But on the idea of agent causation, when I *cause* my volition to move my arm, there is no change I thereby undergo in addition to the change that is the volition itself. So my *causing* my volition is not *itself* a change I undergo. In that sense, then, it is not an event; it has no beginning.

gue that principle I is not violated, even though there is no cause of the agent's-causing-her-volition.

The second line of response is to agree that the-agent's-causing-his-volition falls under the expression "has a beginning," and must, therefore, have a cause. Here the free will advocate may distinguish two distinct sorts of causes, depending on whether the agent had and exercised *free will* in causing his volition. Suppose our person is perched on a pedestal and is quite content with his position until the pedestal catches fire, and the excessive heat of the fire forces him to jump from the pedestal.[13] His action is preceded by the volition (act of willing) to jump, which in turn is substance-caused by the agent. Here we may say that the excessive heat, etc., causes the agent to substance-cause his volition.[14] The volition in this case is causally necessitated by prior events (the fire, etc.) and is not produced freely by the agent in virtue of his power of self-determination. Free will in this case has been abridged. Although the agent has a general power of choosing whether to jump or not, on this occasion his power to choose not to jump has been overridden by the prior events and states which causally determine him to will to jump.

Instead of the pedestal catching fire and causing the agent to jump, suppose that someone comes along and gives the agent a *reason* or *motive* to jump. Perhaps he points out that jumping is a healthful activity and that our pedestal percher is very much in need of such exercise. Suppose that our agent then decides that it would indeed be a good thing to jump and does so. One may wonder how this case differs from the last so far as the causation of the agent's bringing about his volition to jump is concerned. In the first case, the fire plays a major causal role; in the second case, the motive to engage in

13. I borrow this example from Chisholm. See his "Comments and Replies," *Philosophia* 7 (1978):626.

14. As I've already noted, Reid believes it is conceptually impossible to cause an agent to substance-cause anything.

the healthful activity of jumping plays a major causal role. And clearly, this is just how the necessitarian Collins would view the matter. Clarke, however, denies that reasons and motives *cause* the agent to act. For, given the assumption (mentioned earlier) he shares with Collins, to so view the matter is to deny free will and free agency. In his response to Collins he stresses that reasons and motives do not cause the action.

> Occasions indeed they (reasons and motives) may be, and are, upon which that substance in man, wherein the self-moving principle resides, freely exerts its active power. But it is the self-moving principle, and not at all the reason or motive, which is the physical or efficient cause of action. When we say, in vulgar speech, that motives or reasons *determine* a man; it is nothing but a figure or metaphor. It is the man that freely determines himself to act.[15]

But if reasons and motives do not cause the agent to cause his volition, what then is the cause of the-agent's-causing-his-volition? The answer, I believe, must again be the agent himself. What we must suppose is that if the agent causes his volition by virtue of his power of self-determination (that is, as an exercise of free will), then he *thereby causes* each member of a hierarchy or series of events, each more complex than its predecessor: the volition, the agent's causing his volition, the agent's causing his causing his volition, etc. Each member of the hierarchy or series is caused by the agent by virtue of his causing the volition.

Thus far, I have tried to elucidate the view of the agent implied by the free will position, particularly as championed by Clarke. When the agent exercises his free will and performs an action freely, we must suppose first that the agent's volition is not caused by any prior event within or without the

15. *Works* 4:723.

agent; it has as its immediate cause the person whose volition it is. To the question, "What causes the agent to cause his volition?", two different answers can be given. The first answer is that *nothing* causes the agent to cause his volition. Consistent with this answer, the free will advocate must say that the-agent's-causing-his-volition is not an event or a thing that has a beginning. In denying that it has a cause, therefore, the free will advocate does not violate the principle that whatever has a beginning has a cause. Moreover, she may hold that there is a noncausal explanation of the-agent's-causing-his-volition, an explanation in terms of reasons and motives.

The second answer allows that there is a cause of the-agent's-causing-his-volition. If the agent's free will is abridged, the cause will be some prior event such as the fire heating the pedestal so as to cause the agent to jump. If the agent acts through his self-determining power, then the cause of the agent's causing his volition is the same as the cause of his volition: the agent himself. Again, though, we may *explain* why the agent caused his volition by citing not the cause (the agent) but the noncausal factors (reasons and motives) that occasioned the agent to do freely what he did.

We've seen that the first argument from causality against free will rests on the mistaken assumption that the free will position holds volitions to be uncaused events. Once this mistake is acknowledged, however, the argument can be redirected at the view that the agent causes his volition. For either the agent is caused to cause his volition or he is not. If he is, then what becomes of free will? If he is not, then principle I is violated. What we have seen, however, is that the libertarian can avoid this dilemma. On the one hand, he can hold that the agent causes his volition, causes himself to cause his volition, causes himself to cause himself to cause his volition, etc., thus satisfying principle I without abridging free will. Alternatively, the libertarian can argue that the agent's causing his volition is not an event and, therefore, does not fall under the scope of principle I. Since neither of these responses is obviously incoherent or false, our judgment must be that the first argument from causality against free will is less than successful.

The second argument for the conclusion that we are necessary agents and therefore lack free will adds a second principle to the basic principle of the first argument (whatever begins to be has a cause). The second principle is that *every cause is a necessary cause.* The first principle assures us that actions and volitions have causes. Given the second principle, we can infer that actions and volitions have necessary causes. But if all our actions and volitions have necessary causes, then—given the causes—it was not possible for us to refrain from those volitions and actions; we are necessary agents.

A necessary cause is a cause such that, given its existence, the effect necessarily follows. Causes, on this view, *cannot* exist without their effects. Once the cause exists, its effect *must* immediately follow

The second principle was set forth clearly by Hobbes in his controversy with Bishop Bramhall:

> I hold that to be a sufficient cause, to which nothing is wanting that is needful to the producing of the effect. The same is also a necessary cause: for if it be possible that a sufficient cause shall not bring forth the effect, then there wanted somewhat which was needful to the producing of it; and so the cause was not sufficient. But if it be impossible that a sufficient cause should not produce the effect, then is a sufficient cause a necessary cause: for that is said to produce an effect necessarily, that cannot but produce it. Hence it is manifest, that whatsoever is produced, is produced necessarily: for whatsoever is produced, hath had a sufficient cause to produce it, or else it had not been. And therefore also voluntary actions are necessitated.[16]

16. Thomas Hobbes, "The Questions Concerning Liberty, Necessity and Chance," 5:380.

Clearly, if our actions and volitions are caused and their causes are necessary causes—as, given our second principle, they must be—then, given those causes, the volitions and actions could not have failed to occur. But if they could not have failed to occur, then—given the causes—it was not in the power of the agent to will or act otherwise. Hence, the agent is a necessary agent.

The mistake in the first argument against free will was the assumption that the free will position could not accept the principle that whatever has a beginning has a cause. No such mistake is made in the second argument. The libertarians cannot accept the view that the cause of the free volition to do X is a *necessary cause* of that volition. For, according to the free will position, the agent herself causes her volition to do X but could have caused a different volition, the volition, say, to refrain from doing X (or, at least, *not* caused the volition to do X). And in saying that the agent could have caused a different volition, the free will advocate does not mean she could have *if* she had different motives or were in different circumstances, etc. He means that given identical motives, circumstances, etc., the agent could have caused a different volition. So, unlike the response to the first argument, the free will advocate must deny the necessitarian principle that every cause is a necessary cause. Some causes produce effects without being under a necessity to produce those effects.

In responding to Collins's argument (cited above), Clarke rightly sees that the issue between them lies not in the principle that whatever has a beginning must have a cause but in the second principle that every cause is a necessary cause. His response is that the term 'necessary cause' is ambiguous. In one sense the principle is true but trivial. In a second sense (Collins's), the principle begs the question against the free will position.

> The Fallacy of this Argument lies in the Words, *necessary Cause,* 'Tis true that *whatever has a Beginning, must have a Cause.* 'Tis

> true also, that *every Cause is a necessary Cause;* that is, that every adequate efficient Cause, when it is *supposed to operate,* cannot but *produce the Effect,* of which it is at the Time an adequate efficient Cause. But this is saying nothing more, than that any thing *must needs be,* when it *is supposed that it is.* Which is nothing to the Question about Liberty and Necessity. For the *free self-moving Power,* when it is *supposed to exert itself,* cannot but *produce that Motion or Action,* of which it is at that Time the immediate efficient Cause. If I mistake not therefore, this Argument . . . is entirely founded upon the *Supposition,* that there neither is nor can be in Nature any such thing as a *self-moving Power* at all.[17]

The sense in which Clarke admits the principle that every cause is a necessary cause is somewhat difficult to make out. Perhaps what he means is this: The agent is the cause of the effect that is his volition. He is not a necessary cause of that effect since he may exist in just the same circumstances and produce a different action or none at all. But if we suppose not just the agent but the agent's *operation* (the exertion of his power) in producing that action, then we can say we have a necessary cause of the action. But this is trivial, since it is logically impossible that an efficient cause should exert its power to produce an effect and the effect not be produced.

Whatever we make of Clarke's sense of 'necessary cause' in which he finds the second principle acceptable, it is clear that he thinks the agent himself is the cause of his volition but is not a necessary cause in the sense of a cause that cannot exist without producing its effect. The agent is the cause of his volition but could have been the cause of a different volition, without any change of his state or circumstances.

Collins gives a brief argument for the principle that every cause is a necessary cause. He says that if causes are not necessary causes then they "are not suited to or are indifferent to effects."[18] In defense of the free will position, however, we

17. *Works* 4:729.
18. *Human Liberty,* 58.

can distinguish two senses in which a cause may be indifferent (unsuited) to a particular effect. In the first sense it is indifferent if it has no power to bring about or prevent that effect. In the second sense it is indifferent if it can exist without bringing about that effect. In denying that the cause of a volition is a necessary cause, the free will advocate is committed to its being indifferent to the effect (the volition) in the second sense, but not in the first sense.

Collins concludes his brief argument by stating: "And therefore a cause not suited to the effect, and no cause; are the same thing."[19] If a cause is indifferent to an effect in the first sense, then it is indeed no cause at all of that effect. But if a cause is indifferent to an effect in the second sense, it does not follow that it is not a cause of that effect. Indeed, on the free will position, the agent may produce a volition, be the cause of it, even though he (the cause) could exist without producing that volition. Collins's argument, therefore, fails. Although the denial of necessary causes implies the existence of causes that are indifferent in the second sense, this indifference doesn't preclude these causes from producing the effects in question.

A similar difficulty is contained in Hobbes's argument for necessary causes. A sufficient cause, says Hobbes, is something to which nothing is wanting that is needful to the producing of the effect. But the expression 'nothing is needful for C to produce E' is ambiguous. It may mean (1) that C, without the addition of anything else, has the *power* to produce E, or it may mean (2) that C, without the addition of anything else, will necessarily produce E. That Hobbes takes it in sense (2) is clear from his remark: "for if it be possible that a sufficient cause shall not bring forth the effect, then there wanted somewhat which was needful to the producing of it; and so the cause was not sufficient."[20]

19. *Human Liberty,* 59.
20. *English Works* 5:380.

Given Hobbes's understanding of the phrase 'nothing is needful for C to produce E,' it is clear that every *sufficient* cause is a *necessary* cause. But why must everything that is produced have a sufficient cause in Hobbes's sense? Why cannot a volition have a cause that produces it, having the power to do so but producing it without necessity? Hobbes's answer is: "for whatsoever is produced hath had a sufficient cause to produce it, or else it had not been."[21] But this answer begs the question at issue between Hobbes and the libertarians. It simply states that it is impossible that something be produced by a cause that has the power to produce it but can exist without producing it.

In agreeing with Clarke that the Collins-Hobbes arguments beg the question against the free will position, I don't mean to suggest that these arguments are intrinsically bad, only that they cannot (should not) be convincing for someone who holds the free will position. Whether these arguments are intrinsically good or bad depends, I believe, on what is logically included in the concept of a cause. Specifically, it depends on whether the *concept* of a cause includes the idea of a *necessary connection* with whatever is produced by that cause.

That Hobbes and Collins hold that there is a necessary connection between a cause and its effect is clear. Indeed, unless I misread them, they hold that the necessity in question is *logical.* That is, if A causes B it is logically impossible that A should exist but B not exist or not be produced by A. Thus Hobbes concludes that the free will position with its agent who produces an effect but *can* not produce that effect is a *contradictory* position. "Lastly, I hold that the ordinary definition of a free agent, namely, that a free agent is that, which when all things are present which are needful to produce the effect, can nevertheless not produce it, implies a contradic-

21. *English Works* 5:300.

tion, and is nonsense; being as much as to say, the cause may be sufficient, that is, necessary, and yet the effect not follow."[22]

Few, nowadays, would follow Hobbes and Collins in viewing the necessary connection of a cause to its effect as *logical.* Necessary connection remains but is seen as *causal* or *physical* necessity, rather than logical. Given a cause and given the appropriate law of nature, it follows logically that the effect will occur. But a law of nature is not a conceptual truth, so there is no *contradiction* in supposing the cause to exist without the effect being produced. But causal or physical necessity is of no help to the free will advocate. For it is not in the agent's power to alter the laws of nature. So, if every cause necessitates (physically or causally) its effect, then—given the cause—it will not be in the agent's power to prevent its effect. Hence, if the agent is the cause of his volition to do X, then—given the cause—the agent does not have the power to bring about some other volition; the agent is a necessary cause of his volition.

The libertarian is committed to the existence of causes (agents) that are true causes of certain effects (volitions) but are such that their effects are neither logically nor physically *necessitated* by them. He may well admit, and generally does so, that apart from agent causes, causes do physically (or logically) necessitate their effects. But to be an agent, to have the power of self-motion, is to have the power to produce a certain volition and the power to produce a contrary volition (or the power *not* to produce that volition), *all other circumstances and causes remaining the same.* As we've seen, this view is inconsistent with the view that causes necessitate (logically or causally) their effects. Should we therefore judge it to be in-

22. *English Works* 5:385. Concerning the death of Caesar, Collins remarks: "Whereas let them suppose all the same circumstances to come to pass that did precede his death; and then it will be as impossible to conceive (if they think justly) his death could have come to pass anywhere else, as they conceive it impossible for two and two to make six." *Human Liberty,* 165–6.

coherent? This depends, as I noted earlier, on whether the *concept* of a cause includes the idea of a necessary connection with whatever is produced by that cause. On this question, our intuitions may differ. But I, for one, cannot see that being necessarily connected to its effect is a part of our concept of cause, rather than a very entrenched belief we have about causes.[23] I propose, therefore, to treat the idea of an agent who is the free cause of his volition as a coherent idea.

If every cause is a necessary cause, then we must reject the view that agents may produce contrary effects without any alteration in themselves or their circumstances. In holding that the *concept* of cause does not include the idea of a necessary connection to its effect, I am not deciding this issue in favor of the advocates of free agent causes. It may be true that every cause physically or causally necessitates its effect. Indeed, if every cause and effect falls under an appropriate law of nature, then effects are physically necessary, given their causes—in which case agents are not free causes of their effects. My point is that the truth of the claim that every cause is a necessary cause does not *follow* simply from our concept of cause. If this is so, then, although every cause *may* be a necessary cause, Hobbes and Collins have failed to establish the principle that causes are necessary causes. The second argument for necessary agents may be sound, but since its crucial premise (every cause is a necessary cause) is unsupported, the free will advocate is at liberty to reject it.

Neither of the two arguments from causality successfully shows that humans are necessary agents, that we lack the liberty of will Clarke and others claim we possess. Had their view of free will been shown to be inconsistent with the principle that whatever has a beginning has a cause, Clarke and his

23. It is very difficult to present arguments for this view. Some considerations in its favor, however, may be found in G. E. M. Anscombe's inaugural lecture at Cambridge University, "Causality and Determinism" (Cambridge: Cambridge University Press, 1971), and in Peter van Inwagen, *An Essay on Free Will* (Oxford: Oxford University Press, 1983), 138–42.

party would have been in serious trouble. For that principle was fundamental to their arguments for the existence of God. Indeed, for the extreme rationalistic theologians like Clarke, in contrast to moderate rationalists like Edmund Law and Thomas Reid, much stronger principles of causality and explanation were essential to their theological arguments.[24] But the principle that every event has a necessary cause has no place in their rationalistic theology, either extreme or moderate. Clarke, Law, Reid, and the others are free to reject that causal principle.

In this chapter we have looked with care at two objections to libertarianism, objections that were set forth succinctly and clearly by Anthony Collins. We have also examined these objections in the light of Clarke's responses to them. In doing so, I have sought to elucidate and somewhat extend the theory of agency which lies at the heart of the free will position advocated by Clarke. My belief—not defended in this chapter—is that Clarke's view of free will and agency is superior to the views of several of the other well-known eighteenth-century advocates of the free will position.[25] His response to Collins and his controversy with Leibniz reveal, I believe, a gifted mind struggling to reconcile the free will position with a commitment to very strong principles of causality and explanation, principles he thought essential to any demonstration of the existence and nature of God. It is doubtful, however, that he was successful in this undertaking.[26]

Having looked at Locke's conception of freedom, Clarke's

24. For a discussion of extreme and moderate rationalistic theology see W. L. Rowe, "Rationalistic Theology and Some Principles of Explanation," *Faith and Philosophy* 1 (1984):357–69.

25. Collins provides considerable evidence for this in his review of such proponents of free will as Jean LeClerc, William King, and Bishop Bramhall. See *Human Liberty,* 14–22. For some needed corrections on Collins's account of their views see J. O'Higgins's introduction to Collins's *Human Liberty* in his *Determinism and Freewill,* 25–45.

26. See W. L. Rowe, "Rationalistic Theology and Some Principles of Explanation."

position on agency, and some of the problems about causality that surround (if not drown) the free will position, I believe we have established an adequate context in which to begin our examination of Thomas Reid's theory of freedom and morality.

4

Reid's View of Causation and Active Power

> The name of a cause and of an agent, is properly given to that being only, which, by its active power produces some change in itself, or in some other being.
>
> —Thomas Reid

Perhaps the best way to approach Reid's notion of causation is to seek from his published work and correspondence a set of conditions he would regard as necessary and sufficient for *X caused event e.*[1] I suggest the following:

1. X is a *substance* that had *power* to bring about e.
2. X *exerted* its power to bring about e.
3. X had the *power* to refrain from bringing about e.[2]

1. Several editions of Reid's works are available. Unless stated otherwise, references in this study are to the 1983 printing by Georg Olms Verlag of *The Works of Thomas Reid, D.D.* When Reid is quoted or there is a reference to his works in the text of this study, the numbers immediately following the quotation or reference refer to the pages of this volume.

For a current bibliography of works by and about Reid, as well as a philosophically enlightening study of his entire philosophy, I refer the reader to Keith Lehrer, *Thomas Reid* (London: Routledge and Kegan Paul, 1989).

2. In his June 14, 1785, letter to Dr. James Gregory, Reid remarks: "In the strict and proper sense, I take an efficient cause to be a being who had power to produce the effect, and exerted that power for that purpose" (65). He also says: "Power to produce an effect supposes power not to produce it; otherwise it is not power but necessity, which is incompatible with power taken in the strict sense" (65). In light of this last remark we should note that

Our first point establishes that a cause of an event e is always a substance. Actually, Reid's view is that only intelligent substances possessing active power (that is, agents) can be causes.[3] Inanimate substances, events, motives, laws of nature, etc., therefore, cannot be causes for the simple reason that they are not intelligent beings with active power. To forestall misunderstanding, however, we must note that Reid thought that the words 'cause', 'power', and 'agent' are ambiguous, used both in the sense we are engaged in explicating, the "original, strict and proper" sense, and in what he calls the "lax and popular" sense.[4] In the lax and popular sense of 'cause', 'power', and 'agent', substances lacking intelligence, events, laws of nature, and even motives may be causes.

As we've noted, it is Reid's conviction that only beings endowed with will and understanding are causes in the primary sense of 'cause'. But aren't there inanimate substances that in this primary sense have power to cause events? Doesn't a brick, as opposed to a feather, have the power to shatter a window? And doesn't acid, as opposed to water, have the power to dissolve zinc? Whatever we say about these questions, it is clear that neither the brick nor the acid meets Reid's conditions for being causes of the events mentioned. For neither a brick nor acid meets Reid's third condition, and it is questionable whether either meets the second. When a brick is thrown against a window, is it right to say that the brick then *exerts its power* to shatter the window? Perhaps we can say, somewhat anthropomorphically, that when a piece of zinc is placed in a vat of acid, the acid then *exerts its power* to dissolve

---

the sense of 'power' at work in condition (1) renders condition (3) redundant. However, since 'power' has a sense in which (3) would *not* be redundant, I state it as a separate condition, even though this could be misleading.

3. "I am not able to form a conception how power, in the strict sense, can be exerted without will; nor can there be will without some degree of understanding. Therefore, nothing can be an efficient cause, in the proper sense, but an intelligent being" (65).

4. See his letters to Dr. James Gregory, September 23, 1785 (67), July 30, 1789 (73–74), and (no date) (77–78).

the zinc. But clearly the acid has no power to refrain from dissolving zinc. When the conditions are right, the acid must dissolve the zinc. It isn't up to the acid whether or not the zinc gets dissolved. But to be a cause in the strict and proper sense entails having the power to refrain from bringing about e. So, the brick does not cause the shattering of the window; nor does the acid cause the dissolving of the zinc.

In an important study of Reid's agency theory, E. H. Madden rightly notes that Reid's analysis of agent-causation leaves the physical world devoid of active causes, reducing all physical particulars to the level of passive things.[5] Using Reid's favorite weapon, Madden charges that such a view

> contravenes the dictates of commonsense, a consequence which, according to the Scottish tradition, entails the incorrectness of the analysis. According to Reid, agency has two parts: making an event happen and initiating that event. By virtue of this definition, however, it is impossible to say that any particular in the physical world is active as compared to other ones that are passive, or that any particular is active on some occasions and passive on others. But we do ordinarily say such things, so something must be wrong with the analysis.[6]

Madden emphasizes that Reid's account includes the power to *initiate* an event. I take it that he is referring to the part of Reid's account stressing that the exercise of power is up to the agent. Unlike the acid whose power cannot be exercised unless some circumstance obtains and must be exercised when that circumstance obtains, an agent-cause cannot be made to bring about the event it causes. Hence, when an agent does exercise its power, it initiates a change (event) and doesn't merely automatically transmit some force it received from elsewhere or bring about something because some other

5. E. H. Madden, "Commonsense and Agency Theory," *Review of Metaphysics* 36 (1982):319–41.

6. "Commonsense and Agency Theory," 329.

being or set of circumstances necessitated its exercise of power. So, given that inanimate substances do not initiate changes, they are not agents; they lack active power and are merely passive things. But this view, Madden argues, is paradoxical and against commonsense.

> We say that the atmosphere has the power to crush a tin can that has no air inside, the sea the power to crush the submarine that goes too deep, a stick of dynamite the power to explode when detonated, electric current the power to heat a resistance coil when wired in, and so on. We correspondingly say that the atmosphere, sea, stick of dynamite, and the electric current are powerful particulars, or agents, while the can, submarine, and resistance coil are passive particulars, or patients. The former make something happen upon certain releasing conditions, whereas something happens to the latter; the former does something whereas something is done to the latter. However, while such powerful particulars cause something to happen, they do not initiate events; they require a releasing condition such as pumping air out of the can, the submarine's diving too deep, and wiring in a resistance coil. The releasing conditions are part of the cause and hence the powerful particulars are caused to act; they do not initiate an action. On Reid's view, hence, the powerful particulars would not be agents. The result, however, is paradoxical and contrary to commonsense, since the consequence of his strong view of agency requires us to lump together the atmosphere and tin can, the sea and the submarine, the electric current and the resistance coil as equally passive particulars.[7]

Madden is correct in concluding that on Reid's view of what it is to be a cause in the "strict and proper" sense, the atmosphere, sea, and electric current are not causes at all. For, on Reid's view, the sea has active power to crush a submarine that ventures too deep only if the sea has power not to crush a

7. "Commonsense and Agency Theory," 329–30.

submarine that ventures too deep, only if, that is, it is "up to the sea" whether to exercise its power.[8] But why should this be at all paradoxical? Why should this be against common sense? Wouldn't it be more paradoxical to attribute active power and agency to physical particulars when we know that part of what it is to have active power and agency is for it to be "up to the agent" whether or not to exercise its power? Given what Reid means by the "strict and proper" sense of 'cause', 'power', and 'agency', isn't the conclusion Reid reaches and Madden acknowledges exactly right? Physical particulars are one and all passive, lacking power, agency, and causality.

Of course, if Reid insists that there is *no sense* of 'cause', 'power', and 'agency' in terms of which we can properly describe the atmosphere, the sea, a stick of dynamite, etc., as possessing causal power, as being agents of change, then Madden is surely right in arguing that something is wrong with his view. But, as we noted above, Reid does recognize a sense of these terms—what he calls the "lax and popular" sense—in virtue of which certain inanimate things can be described as causes, as agents possessed of power. In correspondence, after describing the "strict and proper" sense of 'cause', he remarks:

> a cause, in the proper and strict sense, (which, I think, we may call the metaphysical sense,) signifies a being or mind that has power and will to produce the effect. But there is another meaning of the word cause, which is so well authorized by custom, that we cannot always avoid using it, and I think we may call it the physical sense; as when we say that heat is the cause that turns water into vapour, and cold the cause that freezes it into ice. A cause, in this sense, means only something which, by the laws of nature, the effect always follows. I think natural philosophers, when they pretend to shew the *causes* of

8. Similarly for the stick of dynamite. Once it is detonated, the dynamite has no power not to explode. It is not up to the dynamite whether to exercise its power of exploding.

natural phenomena, always use the word in this last sense; and the vulgar in common discourse very often do the same. (67)[9]

So, far from denying that the atmosphere or the sea lack causal power to produce certain effects, it is clear that Reid affirms that they are physical causes and agents.[10] It is a mistake, then, to charge Reid with denying our common-sense claims that some physical particulars have causal powers and can be described as agents in bringing about changes in other things.[11]

Following an account of causal powers by Madden and Harre,[12] we can think of gunpowder as having the capacity or causal power to bring about an explosion. Unlike Reid's agent-cause, it is not up to the gunpowder whether and when its power is exercised. The power of gunpowder to explode is necessarily exercised when it is ignited. So, in addition to its capacity to bring about an explosion, the gunpowder has the liability that its power must be exercised under the condition that it is ignited. On this account, it is the gunpowder itself

9. Reid even notes that Hume is right in holding constant conjunction as important to physical causes. "Between a physical cause and its effect, the conjunction must be constant, unless in the case of a miracle or suspension of the laws of nature. What D. Hume says of causes, in general, is very just when applied to physical causes, that a constant conjunction with the effect is essential to such causes, and implied in the very conception of them" (67).

10. He also notes that in physics the law of nature according to which something is produced is itself often called the cause of that thing. "When a phenomenon is produced according to a certain law of nature, we call the law of nature the cause of that phenomenon; and to the laws of nature we accordingly ascribe power, agency, efficiency. The whole business of physics is to discover, by observation and experiment, the laws of nature, and apply them to the solution of the phenomena: this we call discovering the causes of things. But this, however common, is an improper sense of the word *cause*" (66).

11. For a related criticism of Madden's point see R. F. Stalley, "Causality and Agency in the Philosophy of Thomas Reid," *The Philosophy of Thomas Reid,* ed. M. Dalgarno and E. Matthews (Dordrecht: Kluwer Academic Publishers, 1989), 275–76.

12. R. Harre and E. H. Madden, *Causal Power* (Totowa, N.J.: Roman and Littlefield, 1975).

that is to be cited as the cause of the explosion. And my point in defense of Reid is that there is nothing in this account that is precluded by his view of causation. All that his view implies is that the gunpowder is not an agent-cause, a cause in the "strict and proper" sense.

What is perhaps true is that under the influence of seventeenth- and eighteenth-century physics Reid was more likely to talk of a law of nature or an event (the igniting of the gunpowder) as the cause of the explosion. For by this time scientists were moving away from explanations of events in terms of the inherent natures of particular substances in favor of explanations in terms of laws of nature and events or states of substances.[13] But it is no part of Reid's analysis of agent-causation to favor the one account over the other.[14] All that he insists is that no inanimate substance and no event or law of nature is an agent-cause in the "strict and proper" sense. And about this matter he is surely right.

Madden's criticism, however, may be turned in a different direction, a direction that may show some genuine disparity between Reid's view of causation and what would be acceptable nowadays. For although Reid acknowledges that inanimate substances, events, laws of nature, and even motives may be causes (in the lax and popular sense), he thought it self-evident that *every event has an agent-cause.* And what this means is that whenever some event or inanimate substance causes some change there must be an agent-cause somewhere in the background that acted in such a way as to assure that the inanimate substance or event would be the physical cause of that change. In a revealing letter to Dr. James Gregory, Reid set forth this view in response to Gregory's own views about causation.

13. See Reid's discussion of the efficient causes of the phenomena of nature (525–27).

14. As Swinburne has argued, scientific explanation can be cast into either form (Richard Swinburne, *The Existence of God* [Oxford: Clarendon Press, 1979], 43–44).

> You deny that of every change there must be an efficient cause, in my sense—that is, an intelligent agent, who by his power and will effected the change. But I think you grant that, when the change is not effected by such an agent, it must have a physical cause—that is, it must be the necessary consequence of the nature and previous state of things unintelligent and inactive.
>
> I admit that, for anything I know to the contrary, there may be such a nature and state of things which have no proper activity, as that certain events or changes must necessarily follow. I admit that, in such a case, that which is antecedent may be called the physical cause, and what is necessarily consequent, may be called the effect of that cause.
>
> I think also, and I believe you agree with me, that every physical cause must be the work of some agent or efficient cause. Thus, that a body put in motion continues to move till it be stopped, is an effect which, for what I know, may be owing to an inherent property in matter; if this be so, this property of matter is the physical cause of the continuance of the motion; but the ultimate efficient cause is the Being who gave this property to matter. (73–74)

It is one thing to accept Reid's claim that we view ourselves as agent-causes of many of our actions. For this is nothing more than to believe that it was in our power to cause these actions, that we exerted this power, and that it was in our power not to cause them. But it is another thing to accept his claim that every event in the universe is the immediate or ultimate result of the action of an intelligent being. Some would claim that events occur in nature that have no cause at all, neither an agent-cause nor what Reid calls a physical cause. Others who cling to some sort of rationalistic picture of things would insist that every event must have either a physical cause or an agent-cause. But why insist with Reid that agent-causation is ultimate and that every event must have an agent-cause? I must confess that I cannot see anything in this question that is ridiculous or absurd. Of course, if we begin with the belief that there is a first agent, an intelligent being who creates and governs the world, I think we can see how plausible it then would be to think that for every change in nature there is an agent somewhere in the background that causes it. But apart from such a prior belief, it is difficult to see—at least without a good deal of reflection—why some change couldn't occur without there being an intelligent being who caused (immediately or remotely) that change to occur. And we must remember that Reid did not reason to this principle from the belief that there is a God, a first agent. On the contrary, he used the principle as a rational basis for establishing the existence of a first agent. The principle itself, he thought, requires no support; it is self-evident.[15] Whether he was right about this is not a question we need pursue here. For the Reidian view that moral responsibility and free action require that we be agent-causes is logically separable from the metaphysical thesis that every event has an agent-cause. But since this metaphysical thesis is so central to his thinking, it would be misleading to ignore its place in his philosophy and its connection with his theory of freedom and responsibility.

Reid, Samuel Clarke, and other free will advocates used the expression 'efficient cause' for a cause that satisfies Reid's three conditions. Reid used the expression 'physical cause' mainly for events (or things) that are connected to their effects by a law of nature. (To simplify matters, I will take Reid's physical causes to be events connected to their effects by a law of nature.) From his remarks it is clear that Reid believes that efficient causes and physical causes are not two species of a common genus. An efficient cause is a substance that exercises its power to produce an effect, having the power not to produce that effect. A physical cause is an event whose effect follows by virtue of a law of nature. In deference to contemporary usage, I will henceforth use the expression 'agent-cause' for any cause that satisfies Reid's three conditions, and

15. "That every event must have a cause in this proper sense I take to be self-evident" (65). Reid also held the principle to be a necessary truth.

I will use 'event-cause' for (our simplification of) Reid's physical causes.[16] An agent-cause is a cause in what Reid calls the strict and proper sense; an event-cause is a cause in what Reid calls the lax and popular sense.[17]

When the libertarians affirmed the principle that every event has a cause they meant that *every event has an agent-cause.*[18] They did not believe that *every event has an event-cause.* For, on their view, a *free* volition has no event-cause, although it does have an agent-cause. Since they believed that free volitions occur and are events, they were committed to rejecting the principle that every event has an event-cause.

Reid sometimes divides up the principle that every event has a cause into two parts, depending on whether the event in question is the coming into existence of a substance or some change in an existing substance. Thus he remarks: "Every thing that begins to exist, must have a cause of its existence, which had power to give it existence. And every thing that undergoes any change, must have some cause of that change" (603). Clearly, if something comes into existence, its agent-cause must be something distinct from it that exerted its

16. When the context makes it clear which sort of cause is being discussed, I will sometimes just use the word 'cause', leaving it to the reader to determine whether the cause in question is an agent-cause or an event-cause.

17. It is remarkable that in two hundred years our view of causation has so shifted that what for Reid was rather mysterious (event-causation) now seems commonplace, and what for Reid was so commonplace (agent-causation) is viewed by many as obscure, if not unintelligible. After reviewing some objections of present-day philosophers to agent-causation, Alan Donagan remarks: "These objections uncannily reverse the objections Reid made in the eighteenth century against event-causation. Reid pointed out that the necessity possessed by the laws of Newtonian physics was so mysterious that Newton himself indignantly denied that he thought it causal, whereas for centuries the model of causality had been that of the relation of an agent to his actions, and above all, that of the divine agent to his creative actions. . . . In terms of this, the original notion of cause, Reid complained that the post-Newtonian concept of event-causation was improper and obscure" ("Chisholm's Theory of Agency," *Essays on The Philosophy of Roderick M. Chisholm,* ed. Ernest Sosa [Amsterdam: Rodopi, 1979], 218).

18. See Reid, 627.

power to produce the thing that came into existence. When something undergoes a change, however, the agent-cause of that change is either the thing itself or some other being. "In the *first* case it is said to have *active power,* and to *act,* in producing that change. In the *second* case it is merely *passive,* or is *acted upon,* and the active power is in that being only which produces the change" (603).

When we turn to examine the world of nature with Reid's causal principle in mind, we soon are at a loss to discover the agent-causes of events. We see objects undergoing changes, but we don't see causation and power. Primitive people, Reid suggests, simply projected their own capacity for agency onto these natural objects, viewing the objects themselves as the agent-causes of the changes they undergo. They believed that sun, moon, stars, earth, air, and water have understanding and active power. (Reid quotes with favor the Abbé Raynal's remark, "Wherever they see motion which they cannot account for, there they suppose a soul" [605].) This view, of course, had long since been abandoned. Reid acknowledges, however, that little progress has been made in discovering the real agent-causes of the phenomena of nature (526). In its place have arisen a knowledge of event-causes and a knowledge of the laws of nature relating an event-cause to its effect. Such knowledge serves well our practical needs of prediction and control; but the system of event-causation, Reid believes, is understandable only in terms of the more basic system of agent-causation. The laws of nature, on his view, must be understood as *rules* established by some agent for the agent-production of the events related by the laws.

> The *physical laws of nature* are the rules according to which the Deity commonly acts in his natural government of the world; and whatever is done according to them, is not done by man, but by God, either immediately or by instruments under his direction. These laws of nature neither restrain the power of the Author of nature, nor bring him under any obligation to do

> nothing beyond their sphere. He has sometimes acted contrary to them, in the case of miracles, and, perhaps, often acts without regard to them, in the ordinary course of his providence. Neither miraculous events, which are contrary to the physical laws of nature, nor such ordinary acts of the Divine administration as are without their sphere, are impossible, nor are they *effects without a cause.* God is the cause of them, and to him only they are to be imputed. (628)

The point to note here is this. In the "lax and popular" sense, we may cite the law of gravitation as the cause for an object's falling to the ground. Reid accepts this but insists that a law of nature is not a being with intelligence and will and therefore cannot be the agent-cause of the object's falling to the ground. The ultimate agent-cause of the phenomenon is God (or some other agent with sufficient power), the law of nature being nothing more than a rule the agent has established and chosen to follow in causing such things to happen. Although all this may strike us as odd, it should be understandable how such a view of a law of nature would take shape if one starts with the metaphysical thesis that there must be an agent-cause for every event.[19]

Acknowledging that in the theater of nature we see many effects that require as their cause an agent endowed with active power, an agent whose causal activity is "behind the scene," Reid concludes that we have no great need for such knowledge. "It is only in human actions, that may be imputed for praise or blame, that it is necessary for us to know who is the agent; and in this, nature has given us all the light that is necessary for our conduct" (527). We do know, Reid contends,

19. It is worth noting that Reid thought Newton to have a similar view. Thus he remarks: "The grandest discovery ever made in natural philosophy, was that of the law of gravitation, which opens such a view of our planetary system that it looks like something divine. But the author of this discovery was perfectly aware, that he discovered no real cause, but only the law or rule, according to which the unknown cause operates" (527).

that we are the agent-causes of those of our actions for which we are responsible. But even here we may depend on causal factors we do not ourselves produce. If I will to shoot someone, I may view myself as immediately causing my act of aiming the gun and pulling the trigger. But I don't cause gunpowder to have its explosive power. I don't, as Reid notes, give "to the flint and steel the power to strike fire." At best, I may initiate a member (pulling the trigger) of a causal chain that results in a bullet striking a person. The existence of the causal chain, however, is not due to my causal power. Reid acknowledges that in the strict sense I am not the sole agent-cause of my act of shooting the person. How then can I be responsible for this act? I am responsible because I am the *moral cause* of the action, even if I am not the sole agent-cause of it. For I will to shoot the person believing that my action of killing him depends upon my will (528).

Reid distinguishes between the *immediate* and the *remote* effects of an agent's exertion of active power. The immediate effects are certain movements of our body and certain directions of our thought that we produce by our will. Thus, if I move my arm by willing to do so, the act of moving my arm is an "immediate effect," as are other bodily motions I cause by willing them. Remote effects are actions we produce only by means of some immediate effect. For example, we shoot the man (willing and intending to do so) only by producing some motion in our own body (pulling the trigger). As we noted, Reid acknowledges that in shooting the man we depend on causal connections in nature that we do not produce. But because we intend that action, we are the *moral* cause of our shooting the man even though we are not, strictly speaking, the agent-cause (or the sole agent-cause) of that action. Indeed, even in the case of an immediate effect, moving my arm, it can be doubted that I am, strictly speaking, the agent-cause. For the arm moves because of muscle contractions that are in turn produced by certain impulses in my nervous system. So it appears that in willing to move my arm I am not, in the strict sense, the agent-cause (or sole agent-cause) of my action of moving my arm. Reid remarks:

> That there is an established harmony between our willing certain motions of our bodies, and the operation of the nerves and muscles which produces those motions, is a fact known by experience. This volition is an act of the mind. But whether this act of the mind have any physical effect upon the nerves and muscles; or whether it be only an occasion of their being acted upon by some other efficient, according to the established laws of nature, is hid from us. So dark is our conception of our own power when we trace it to its origin. (528)

I take it that Reid thinks that either our volition to raise our arm has some inherent property in virtue of which it produces the changes in our nerves and muscles, or there is a law of nature to that end, the results being due to the action of some agent other than ourselves. (As we've seen, even if we suppose that the volition has such an inherent property, on Reid's view the true cause of the movements in the nerves is the intelligent being who gave that property to our volitions.) In any case, he draws the same conclusion as he does for the remote effects of our volitions. "The man who knows that such an event depends upon his will, and who deliberately wills to produce it, is, in the strictest moral sense, the cause of the event; and it is justly imputed to him, whatever physical causes may have concurred in its production" (528).

Reid's basic view is that what an agent causes are her volitions and the actions that are causally initiated by her volitions. In the strict sense the agent may not be the agent-cause (or the sole agent-cause) of the actions, but her responsibility remains in that she can be said to be their *moral cause.* Are all actions initiated by volitions? Reid thought not. Volitions require an intentional object, the action willed, and therefore require some degree of understanding of the thing willed. When the newborn infant sucks at the breast, it acts without understanding and therefore without will. When a mature person with understanding and will reaches out spontaneously to break a sudden fall, the person acts without first willing the act. But it is clear that Reid sees the act of will as the essential ingredient in the class of actions for which the agent is morally accountable.[20]

Are all the actions causally initiated by the agent's willing them actions for which the agent bears moral responsibility? Reid again thought not. For the agent's volition may be necessitated by prior events and circumstances. If so, then the agent did not agent-cause his act of will and may not bear moral responsibility for the performance of the action willed. If the flood of passion causally necessitates the volition to do X, then the person was not the agent-cause of his volition to do X. Such a person wills of necessity what he wills—the volition is event-caused by the occurrence of his passions; it is not agent-caused by the person, and he therefore is not morally accountable for the action that results from his act of will. He may, however, be accountable for being in a situation where his passions are irresistible.

Following an ancient tradition, Reid divides the influences on the agent into the cool part, reason, and the irrational part, the appetites, desires, and passions. The first he likens to advice which may influence but never diminishes the agent's power to resist. The second is always violent in its influence and invariably diminishes or, if irresistible, overcomes the agent's power to resist. "Arguments, whatever be the degree of their strength, diminish not a man's liberty; they may produce a cool conviction of what we ought to do, and they can do no more. But appetite and passion give an

20. We do hold persons responsible for actions they do not will. But, generally, these actions are done in the course of doing other actions that are willed. Thus, if I will to open my car door and do so, with the result that I knock you off your bicycle, I may be accountable for what I did through culpable ignorance—knocking you off your bicycle—even though I did not will to do it.

impulse to act and impair liberty, in proportion to their strength" (536). If the strength of the passions is such as to overcome the power not to will, then, for the reason given, the act of will is necessitated by prior events and circumstances. The agent is not the cause of his volition. If the passions are not irresistible, then, presumably the agent does cause the volition, but the action is attributed partly to the agent and partly to the passions. The degree to which the action is attributable to the agent is a function of the degree of power the agent has not to will the action. Reid clearly views the power to will (and not to will) as something that may be diminished or overcome (impairment of liberty) by the increasing strength of the passions.

Having given something of a summary of Reid's view of what it is to be an agent-cause (a cause in the "strict and proper sense"), we now need to explore the extent to which a necessitarian could agree with Reid that we are sometimes the agent-cause of our actions. Can a necessitarian consistently view herself as an *agent-cause* of some of her actions? The answer, I believe, is no. To see why this is so, let's begin by returning to our earlier reasoning concerning whether the brick is the agent-cause of the window's breaking, or the acid is the agent-cause of the zinc's dissolving. We decided that neither is the agent-cause of the events in question because (1) the brick does not "exert its power" to break the window—at best it is the instrument of some other force—and (2) neither the brick nor the acid has the power *not* to cause their respective effects when the circumstances are such that they may be said to cause them. When the conditions are right, the acid, for example, must dissolve the zinc. It isn't up to the acid whether to act or not act. So Reid's third condition of what it is to agent-cause an event is not satisfied. Contrast this with the following example. I invite you to write down the word *cause*. Let's suppose that you have the power to do so and that you exert that power with the result that a change in the world occurs: the word *cause* is written on a piece of paper. Here, when we look at Reid's third condition, we believe that it does obtain. We believe that you have the power to refrain from initiating your action of writing down the word *cause.* The acid had no such power of refraining from dissolving the zinc, but you had the power not to bring about your action of writing down the word *cause.* If these things are so, then in this instance you are a true agent-cause of a certain change in the world, for you have the power to bring about that change, you exerted that power by acting, and finally, you had the power not to bring about that change.

While all of this, if true, clearly distinguishes what we believe of persons when they cause some events from what we believe about some nonpersons (the brick, the acid) when we view them as causes of events, we have not yet seen why the necessitarian cannot accept these distinctions and therefore accept the view that we are sometimes, if not often, the agent-causes of events and actions. The problem for the necessitarian comes to the surface when we raise the question of whether the person can be *caused* to agent-cause some event or action. This is the same problem that emerged in Chapter 2 when we considered Clarke's view that a *necessary agent* is a self-contradictory idea. We there tried to rescue the idea of an agent being caused to agent-cause some action or event by suggesting that in such a case the factors that cause the agent to act are internal to the agent: desires, beliefs, and the like. We noted that such a response would be rejected by Clarke on the grounds that the 'agent' would then not *begin* any action or motion; the 'agent', on Clarke's view, would then only be a patient, a subject of changes wrought by earlier things and changes. We responded by saying that Clarke's argument begs the question against the necessitarian. Now, however, we have an additional problem to consider. For it now appears that an agent-cause must not only have the power to *initiate* or bring about some event or action; the agent-cause must also have the power *not* to bring about that event or action.[21] Reid's

21. I suspect that Clarke and Reid do not really differ on the conditions for being an agent-cause. Thus, I'm not suggesting that Reid's 'power not to bring about' is a condition he *adds* to Clarke's view. Reid is simply clearer and

third condition of agent-causation requires that the cause have the power not to bring about the event or action. Suppose an event occurs that causes you to cause something to happen: some boiling water spills on your hand, causing you to drop the pot of boiling water. Now if the spilling of the boiling water on your hand really does cause you to bring about your dropping the pot, if it causally necessitates you to cause your dropping of the pot, then given the spilling of the boiling water on your hand it wasn't in your power not to bring about your dropping the pot. But you are the agent-cause of some change only if it was in your power at the time not to cause that change. This being so, it is quite impossible that anything should ever *cause* you to *agent-cause* some change. For if some event causes you to cause some change, then—given that event—you caused that change of necessity and lacked the power not to cause it. Since having the power not to cause a change is required for you to be the agent-cause of some change, and since being caused to cause some change implies that you cannot refrain from causing that change, it follows that no one can be caused to agent-cause a change. If you are the agent-cause of some change, it follows that you were not caused to agent-cause that change.

The example of "being caused to cause" just given may be questioned as less than a serious attempt to provide an example of being caused to *agent-cause* something. For boiling water on the hand is likely to produce an immediate reflex action on my part of dropping the pot. No exercise of power through an act of will to drop the pot actually occurs. So, while the argument against the possibility of being caused to

---

more complete in his articulation of what it is to be an agent-cause. Unlike Clarke, however, he is more willing to allow for the different senses of the word 'cause.' But so long as we are using 'cause' in the strict and proper sense, he agrees with Clarke that a *necessary agent* is an *impossibility*. "Were it not that the terms *cause* and *agent* have lost their proper meaning, in the crowd of meanings that have been given them, we should immediately perceive a contradiction in the terms *necessary cause,* and *necessary agent*" (607).

agent-cause something may be a good argument, the example is not to the point. To remedy this, consider someone who is being tortured to disclose a secret with which he has been entrusted. Slowly the pain is increased until it reaches a level that is truly unbearable. We will suppose that the pain is so intense that it causes the person to reveal the secret; not by some unintended reflex, but by a decision (an act of will) to reveal the secret and thereby stop the pain. Now, either the intensity of the pain is causally sufficient in the circumstances for the decision to reveal the secret or it is not. If it is, then we can say that our person is caused to reveal the secret. If it is not, then we don't have a suitable example. So let's suppose the former: the intensity of the pain causes our person to reveal the secret. Our question now is whether the person agent-causes his revealing the secret. If so, then we have what we seek: an instance of someone being caused to agent-cause something. But if the intensity of the pain was causally sufficient in the circumstances for his revealing the secret, then—given the pain and the circumstances—the person had no power not to cause himself to reveal the secret. And if the person lacked power *not* to cause himself to reveal the secret, then the person did not agent-cause his revealing the secret. Since being caused to cause A implies that, given the cause, one lacked power not to cause A, it is impossible that a person be caused to agent-cause A.

A necessitarian can hardly respond to this argument by holding that an agent-cause of an event e need not have the power not to cause e. For such a view simply denies the conditions Reid lays down for agent-causation. A more promising necessitarian response, at least initially, is to recognize that the agent-cause of e must have the power *not* to cause e, and to hold, accordingly, that if a person is the agent-cause of some event or action then the person must have had the power *not* to bring about that event or action. As we've seen from our study of Locke, the necessitarian can take this position with respect to *actions* that the agent performs *freely*. For it is a mark of a Lockean free action that the agent had the power not to do it. It was in his power not to do it in the sense that he *could* have refrained from so acting *if he had willed to refrain from so acting.* And the helpful point to be made here for the necessitarian position is that this power not to bring about the event is compatible with the agent being caused to cause the event. For my being causally determined to bring about e does not imply that I *could not* have refrained from bringing about e *if* I had willed not to bring about e.

The (now familiar) response of the libertarian to this necessitarian account is twofold. First, the libertarian denies that the mere fact that I could have refrained from bringing about e *if* I had so willed is sufficient for concluding that it was in my power not to bring about e. It must also be true that it was in my power to will not to bring about e. Second, the libertarian argues that *willing* is also an event that the agent may *cause.* Therefore, if I am the agent-cause of my volition to do some action (say, move my arm) it must be that it was in my power not to cause that volition (act of will). And while the necessitarian may contend that her conditional account of power is applicable to voluntary actions, no such view can be applied at the level of volitions. It is not credible to say that the agent's power not to cause his act of will comes to nothing more than this: the agent could have refrained from bringing about his volition *if* he had willed not to bring it about. Moreover, the necessitarians themselves insist that although we do have power over certain of our actions (the ones done freely), we do not have power over the will itself. As we saw earlier (Chapter 2), the necessitarians concede that libertarian power over the will is incompatible with the causal determination of our volitions by prior events and circumstances. It is no accident, therefore, that the necessitarians tend to locate freedom solely at the level of actions that flow from volitions.[22]

22. Leibniz, as we saw, criticized Locke for failing to provide any account of freedom as applied to the will. But Leibniz's own recommendations fall far short of the libertarian power to will different things when all the causes and circumstances are the same.

It is fair to conclude, I believe, that the necessitarian cannot assent to the view that we are sometimes the agent-cause of our actions, where this is understood to imply that Reid's three conditions are satisfied. She cannot assent because the necessitarian thesis would require that when a person is the agent-cause of some voluntary action, the person is *caused* to agent-cause that action and *caused* to agent-cause the volition leading to that action. But neither view is plausible given Reid's third condition of what it is to be an agent-cause of some event e: having the power not to bring about e.

Although Reid's notion of causation in the "strict and proper sense" (what we have called 'agent-causation') is expressible in a set of three conditions, it's clear that these three conditions do not constitute a proper definition of agent-causation, for each condition embodies the causal notion of 'bringing about.' Whether these conditions can be stated without using such obvious synonyms for 'cause' as 'produce' or 'bring about' is not a matter we need pursue here. What is important to note is that Reid's concept of agent-causation is fundamentally dependent on the notion of active power, the power an agent has to bring about or not bring about a certain event.

Following Locke, Reid argues that our idea of active power is acquired not from changes observed in external things but from our consciousness of changes within ourselves. Reflecting on certain changes in our thoughts, in the motions of our bodies, and, Reid would add, in the determinations of our will (volitions), we are irresistibly led to attribute to ourselves the power to bring about these changes. The changes in thought and bodily motion that we attribute to ourselves are occasioned by our willing them. But to will some change one must understand what is being willed. So power with respect to bringing about changes in our thoughts and the motions of our body is exerted by our willings, and will implies some degree of understanding.

> From this, I think, it follows, that, if we had not will, and that degree of understanding which will necessarily implies, we

could exert no active power, and consequently could have none; for power that cannot be exerted is no power. It follows also, that the active power, of which only we can have any distinct conception, can be only in beings that have understanding and will. (523)

Reid proposes no definition of 'active power.' His view is that this notion, like a good many others, is indefinable. He does, however, make a number of observations and remarks about active power, some of which it will be helpful to have before us.

1. Unlike the operations or activities of the mind (exertions of power), power itself is not something of which we are directly conscious. (512)
2. Power varies in both kind and degree. "Thus a power to fly and a power to reason, are different kinds of power, their effects being different in kind. But a power to carry one hundred weight, and a power to carry two hundred, are different degrees of the same kind." (514)[23]
3. "We cannot conclude the want of power from its not being exerted; nor from the exertion of a less degree of power, can we conclude that there is no greater degree in the subject." (514)
4. Power is an attribute which cannot exist but in some being that is the subject of that attribute. (522)
5. Every change is brought about by some exertion of power, or by the cessation of some exertion of power. (515)
6. The being that produces a change by the exertion of its power is the *cause* of that change. (515)
7. "Power to produce any effect implies power not to produce it." (523)

We will later look at arguments for and against the view that

23. Reid's examples here are curious. Birds have the power to fly; humans do not. Yet he does not think that nonhumans are endowed with active power. Perhaps Reid is himself here lapsing into the "lax and popular" sense of 'power.'

human beings sometimes have active power. For, as we shift to Reid's view of human freedom, it will become clear that for an agent to enjoy such freedom with respect to a certain action is nothing more than for the agent to possess active power with respect to that action. And we will certainly need to look with care at Reid's position concerning these arguments. For the moment, however, we should not pass by Reid's insistence that we all share a *belief* that we possess active power with respect to some of our actions and willings. As he puts it: "All our volitions and efforts to act, all our deliberations, our purposes and promises, imply a belief of active power in ourselves; our counsels, exhortations, and commands, imply a belief of active power in those to whom they are addressed" (517). If I deliberate about whether to mow the lawn today, I must *believe* that mowing the lawn is in my power, that it is up to me whether or not I mow the lawn. It could be that I am mistaken in this belief. Someone may have stolen my lawn mower; while sitting and deliberating, without my knowledge I may have suffered a nervous disorder that has rendered my legs useless, etc. So genuine deliberation can occur even though mowing the lawn today is not within my power. But unless I believe that it is in my power, I cannot deliberate.[24] Since it is an obvious fact that we deliberate, make promises, etc., then, whether we have active power or not, we are constantly in the position of believing that many actions are within our power.

24. Compare Richard Taylor, *Action and Purpose* (Englewood Cliffs, N.J.: Prentice-Hall, 1966), 171: "One can only deliberate about what he believes to be within his own power. Thus, 'I am deliberating whether Smith shall be reprieved' entails 'I believe it to be within my power alone to reprieve Smith.'"

This position, like Reid's, may be too strong. Perhaps all that is entailed by my deliberation about whether to mow the lawn today is that I *not* believe that mowing the lawn is not in my power. In the dispositional sense of 'believe,' however, I suspect Reid is correct. If I were genuinely deliberating about whether to mow the lawn and the question were raised as to whether I believe it is within my power to mow it, I could hardly respond by saying I'm unsure whether I do believe it.

Now a necessitarian would like to agree with Reid on this point. As he would say (and Reid at times talks in a similar fashion), what is in our power is *what depends on our will.* Walking is in our power; the circulation of our blood is not. What is the difference? The first is subject to our will; the second is not. As Reid himself admits: "This [being subject to our will] is the infallible criterion by which we distinguish . . . what is in our power from what is not" (524). Since we sometimes deliberate about whether to walk, whether to mow the lawn, etc., we believe these things must be subject to our will. If we will to do them we can do them, and if we will not to do them we can refrain from doing them. This and no more is what it is for such things to be in our power. Thus, it would seem that the necessitarian, no less than Reid, can hold that we sometimes deliberate about what we shall do, that deliberation implies a belief in active power, and even that we do have such active power. For, as we have just seen, active power extends to those activities that we can do if we will and can refrain from doing if we will.

Given this conception of active power (as extending only to activities that are subject to the will), it is again clear that inanimate objects (the brick, the acid) really lack active power. Earlier we noted that the brick and the acid lack power not to bring about what they cause. When the conditions are right the brick cannot not shatter the window, nor (when the conditions are right) is it up to the acid whether or not to dissolve the zinc. Now we can note in addition that beings or things have *active power* only over *what is subject to their wills.* Clearly this is an additional reason for denying active power to inanimate objects. But it should also be clear that Reid's view of active power requires not just power over *what is subject to our wills* but also power over *the determinations of our will.* This is what we earlier concluded when we tested the necessitarian's conditional account of power against Reid's view of power as extending not only to actions willed but also to our willings of those actions. For Reid (1) simply denies that we can have power with respect to what we will do if we do not have power over our willings, and (2) argues that our willings, no less than our willed actions, are events or changes that occur in the agent. They, too, therefore, must be agent-caused by some agent—either the agent whose willings they are or some other agent. If the former, then the actions subject to the will are within the agent's power. If the latter, then the action flowing from the volition is not in the agent's power, for her will is not in her power. With respect to (1), Reid advances a rather interesting argument that we will later examine in some detail. "For to say that what depends upon the will is in a man's power, but the will is not in his power, is to say that the end is in his power, but the means necessary to that end are not in his power, which is a contradiction" (602). And with respect to (2), Reid makes it abundantly clear that a change, "whether it be of thought, or will, or of motion," is an *effect.* As such, it must be caused by the power of an agent (603). "I consider the determination of the will as an effect. This effect must have a cause which had power to produce it; and the cause must be either the person himself, whose will it is, or some other being" (602).

Clearly, then, if the volition, no less than the action willed, is something that is agent-caused, we cannot hold that only willed actions are in our power; we must also hold that the determinations of the will are in our power. For if they be not within our power, then we cannot be the cause of them. And if we do not cause our volitions, some other agent must. But if our volitions are caused by some other agent, then that agent is the proper cause of our volitions and the actions that flow from them.

The charitable modern reader may see the above defense of the ideas of agent-causation and active power as plausible within the context of the *eighteenth-century* controversy between the libertarians and the necessitarians. After all, the notion of agent-causation was still prominent relative to the competing notion of event-causation. Although Hume, Priestley, and others embraced the notion of event-causation, there was still a viable intellectual tradition in place, a tradition in which the important causes in the world are agents who bring things about by virtue of exercising active power. Granted the prominence of this tradition, it is only reasonable to take full account of the ideas of agent-causation and active power in both framing and evaluating the libertarian-necessitarian controversy. But surely, the modern reader will continue, Reid's notions of causation and power are at best quaint relics to the twentieth-century mind. Nowadays, the notion of event-causation completely dominates our understanding of how and why things happen as they do. One event is explained as the causal product of an earlier event when there is a law of nature properly relating the two. Although we continue to speak of substances (particular agents) as causes, the learned regard such claims as reducible to claims about events involving those substances (or agents) as causing other events.[25] Surely, then, we can no longer seriously credit Reid's theory of freedom, founded as it is on a charming but no longer variable view of causation.

For the most part in what follows I will put to one side the objection just raised. In the last two chapters, however, we will return to it when we consider whether Reid's libertarianism is ultimately committed to a mysterious, unique causal connection between a substance (the agent) and an event (the agent's volition to perform some action).

25. See, for example, C. D. Broad, "Determinism, Indeterminism, and Libertarianism," *Ethics and the History of Philosophy* (London: Routledge and Kegan Paul, 1952), 195–217.

5

Reid's Conception of Freedom

> If the person was the cause of that determination of his own will, he was free in that action, and it is justly imputed to him, whether it be good or bad.
>
> —Thomas Reid

We've seen that the heart of the libertarian objection to the sort of freedom (Lockean freedom) embraced by the necessitarians is that it fails to extend freedom to the will itself. We should expect, therefore, that Reid's account of free action will include not only power to act *if* we will but also power over the will itself. Here is Reid's account:

> By the *liberty* of a moral agent, I understand, a power over the determinations of his own will.
>
> If, in any action, he had power to will what he did, or not to will it, in that action he is free. But if, in every voluntary action, the determination of his will be the necessary consequence of something involuntary in the state of his mind, or of something in his external circumstances, he is not free; he has not what I call the liberty of a moral agent, but is subject to necessity. (599)

It is helpful, I believe, to divide Reid's view of freedom into two theses: a negative thesis and a positive thesis. The negative thesis is this: if some action (inaction) of ours is free, then our decision or act of will to do that action (not to do it) cannot have been causally necessitated by any prior events, whether they be internal or external. If I have a machine hooked up to your brain in such a manner that my flip of a switch causally necessitates your decision to get up and walk across the room, it follows that you are not free in your action of getting up and walking across the room. In this case your decision to do that action is causally necessitated by some prior *external* event, the flipping of the switch. On the other hand, if your decision to do the act was causally necessitated by your desires and circumstances (matters that are involuntary), then the causally necessitating event is *internal,* and the action again is not free. You are free in some action (inaction) only if your decision to do that act (not to do it) is not causally necessitated by any involuntary event, whether internal or external.

All too often, it is assumed that this concept of freedom, which I shall call *Reidian freedom,* consists in nothing more than this negative thesis. And the major objection of the necessitarians to Reidian freedom is based on this assumption. According to Reid, our free acts of will are not caused by any prior events, whether external or internal. And the difficulty with this, so the objection goes, is that it conflicts with the view that every event has a cause, a view that most eighteenth-century philosophers, including Reid, accepted. What this objection reveals, however, is that the necessitarians hold to only one sort of causation, causation by prior events. Thus, once it was denied that our free acts of will are caused by any prior events, the necessitarians concluded that the advocates of Reidian freedom were committed to the view that our free acts of will are totally uncaused events. But, as we saw in the last chapter, Reid, following Samuel Clarke, Edmund Law, and others, believed in another sort of causation, causation by persons or agents. And what they affirmed in their positive thesis is that free acts of will are caused by the agent whose acts they are. Reid, then, no less than the necessitarians, affirmed that all events, including our free acts of will, are caused. As he remarks: "I grant, then, that an effect uncaused is a contradiction, and that an event uncaused is an absurdity. The question that remains is whether a volition, undetermined by motives, is an event uncaused. This I deny. The cause of the volition is the man that willed it" (87).

How are we to understand Reidian freedom of action in comparison with Lockean freedom of action? A natural view to take is that Reidian freedom of action *just is* Lockean freedom of action supplemented by power over the will. What Reid says, however, is this: "If, in any action, he had power to will what he did, or not to will it, in that action he is free." Taken literally, this remark neglects Locke's point that the person must be able not only *to do* what he wills, but also *to refrain* from the action should that be what he wills. Perhaps, however, this is just a slip on Reid's part. Perhaps he really meant to provide an account of a free action that adds the power to will to do or to will not to do to Locke's power to do if we will and power not to do if we will not to do. That this is what Reid meant is suggested by the best work on Reid's account of freedom. Timothy Duggan, for example, advances this account. "For Reid it is not sufficient for a man to be said to have acted freely that he had the power to do what he willed to do, or to refrain from doing what he willed to refrain from; it is further required that he had the power to will to do that thing *and* to will to refrain from doing it as well."[1] Another expression of the view that Reidian freedom is Lockean freedom supplemented by power over the will is the following: "Admitting that without a doubt the ability to do as one wills is a necessary condition of moral freedom, Reid claims that it is not sufficient. Also required is freedom of the will, which is defined as the power an agent has over the determinations of his will."[2]

The standard account of Reidian freedom—Lockean free-

1. "Active Power and the Liberty of Moral Agents," *Thomas Reid: Critical Interpretations,* ed. Stephen F. Barker and Tom L. Beauchamp (Philadelphia: Philosophical Monographs, 1976), 106.

2. Jerome A. Weinstock, "Reid's Definition of Freedom," *Journal of the History of Philosophy* 13, no. 3 (1975):335.

dom supplemented with power over the will—is, I believe, an incorrect interpretation of Reid's view. Before seeing what is wrong with the standard account, however, we need a precise statement of it. In what follows, the first account of freedom ($free_1$) is Locke's. I then state *the standard account* of Reid's notion of free will, using it to state *the standard account* of his view of being free ($free_2$) with respect to an action.

> S is $free_1$ with respect to action A just in case it is in S's power to do A if S should will to do A and in S's power to refrain from doing A if S should will to refrain.

> S has free will with respect to action A just in case it is in S's power to will to do A and in S's power to will to refrain from doing A.

> S is $free_2$ with respect to action A just in case S is $free_1$ with respect to action A and has free will with respect to action A.

Reid tells us that an agent performs an action freely if he had the power "to will what he did, or not to will it." Taking Reid at his word—as I propose to do—two elements in the standard account are noticeably absent. First, Reid does not say that the agent must have been able to do otherwise (or to refrain) if he had willed to do otherwise (or willed to refrain). Second, Reid does not say that the agent must have had the power to will otherwise (or to will to refrain); instead, he speaks of the power *not to will.* Of course, one might say that the first is just an oversight and the second simply a matter of style. What, after all, is the difference between the power to *will to refrain* from doing A and the power *not to will* to do A? I believe the difference is real, but to see the difference we must connect up Reid's account of a free action with his account of causation, and to appreciate the difference we must connect up his account of a free action with his idea of an action for which we are justly held responsible. When we do these two things, we shall be able to see the crucial difference between Reidian freedom and the standard account of Reidian freedom.

Reid tells us that a willed action is free provided you had the power to will it and the power not to will it. Having looked at his view of agent-causation in the last chapter, it is clear that the power to will is the power *to cause* the act of will, and the power not to will is the power *not to cause* the act of will. According to Reidian freedom, therefore, any action we perform as a result of our act of will to do that action is a *free* action provided that we were the agent-cause of the act of will to perform that action. And since to agent-cause an act of will includes the power not to cause it, we can say that every act of will resulting in a *free* action is an act of will we had power to produce and power not to produce.

Later in the chapter in which he introduces the notion of moral liberty, Reid turns to the question of the *causation* of the determination of the will that results in one's action. Pointing out that the determination of the will is an *effect,* he says, consistent with his view that every effect has an agent-cause, that "the cause must be either the person himself, whose will it is, or some other being" (602). He then makes the point that the person's action was *free* provided that he caused his volition to do the action. "If the person was the cause of that determination of his own will, he was free in that action, and it is justly imputed to him, whether it be good or bad" (602).

When we compare the passage just cited with our original passage, in which Reid describes a free action as a voluntary action in which the agent had the power to will it and the power not to will it, we really have no alternative but to understand the power to will and the power not to will as the power *to cause* the volition and the power *not to cause* the volition. A voluntary action done by the agent is an action that the agent willed to do. But an agent can will the action even though he, as agent, is not the cause of that act of will. If the tide of his passions overwhelms him and causes that volition in him, it remains true that he wills the action, but he wills it of necessity, not freely. A voluntary action is a free action if and only if the agent *caused* the volition to do that action. (It is supposed here that a voluntary action is an action that results in a normal way from the agent's willing to perform that action.) It is also true that a voluntary action is a free action if and only if the agent who willed and did it had the power to will it and the power not to will it. Since the power to cause includes the power not to cause, these two accounts are really equivalent. The correct interpretation of Reid's idea of a free action is simply this. An action is free just in case the agent willed to perform it, performed it as a result of willing to perform it, and the agent was the cause of the act of will to perform the action. Since power to cause implies power not to cause, it will be true in any free action that the agent had the power not to cause the act of will (the power not to will the action).

We've taken one step in the direction of seeing that the standard account of Reidian freedom is incorrect. For in linking up Reid's talk of power to will and power not to will with his fundamental notion of agent-causation, we've seen that the only proper interpretation of the power not to will is the power not to cause the act of will in question. But again, one may question whether there is any significant difference between the power not to will and the power to will otherwise (or the power to refrain from willing). To appreciate the significance of the difference, we now need to take the second step and connect up his account of a free action with an action for which we are justly held responsible.

Reid argued that we are morally responsible for our actions and our volitions only if we are free in our actions and willings. On the standard account of Reidian freedom (Lockean freedom with the addition of power over the determinations of the will), an agent acts freely in doing A only if (1) *she could have avoided doing A had she so willed* and (2) *she could have willed to refrain from doing A*. I have suggested that neither of these aspects of the standard account is part of a correct account of

Reidian freedom: the first is absent together, and the second (the power to have willed to refrain from doing A) is wrongly substituted for the power *not to cause* the act of will to do A.[3] The importance of these two differences between the standard account and the correct account becomes apparent when we examine Reid's claim of a logical connection between responsibility and freedom. For there are, I believe, good reasons to doubt the traditional claim that an agent is morally responsible for doing A only if she could have avoided doing A. And there are good reasons to doubt the claim that an agent is morally responsible for doing A only if she could have willed to refrain from doing A (or avoided willing to do A). The significance of the correct account of Reidian freedom is that none of these reasons applies to it.

In distinguishing a voluntary action from a free action, Locke provides the example of a man who wills to stay in a room, not knowing it to be locked. This person acts voluntarily, not freely (that is, with Lockean freedom). But I think we may justly hold such a person responsible even though he would not have been able to avoid staying in the room had he willed not to stay in the room. For although the locked door causally necessitates his not leaving the room, it does not necessitate his *voluntary action* of staying in the room. It was in the agent's power not to cause his volition and therefore in his power not to cause his action of staying in the room. The agent may not be responsible for the state of affairs of his remaining in the room.[4] But the agent may be responsible for *his action* of staying in the room. And if such a person is

3. It is important to distinguish *the power to have willed to refrain from doing A* from *the power not to will to do A*. It is also important to note that the latter includes both *the power to avoid willing to do A* and *the power not to cause the act of will to do A*. As we shall see, these last two are different. One may retain the power not to cause a volition even when one has lost the power to avoid the volition. By 'the power not to will to do A' Reid means 'the power not to cause the act of will to do A.'

4. He may not be responsible because it can be argued that it is the locked door that necessitates his staying in the room.

morally accountable for what he does, moral responsibility does not entail Reidian freedom *if* Reidian freedom is correctly understood as Lockean freedom with addition of power over the will. As we've noted, however, there is nothing in Reid's account to suggest that the agent must have had the power to do otherwise had he so willed. What Reid says is that if a person wills to perform some action and does so, then he performs that action freely provided he had the power *not to will* to do that action. The person in Locke's example acts freely in staying (on Reid's account) because it was in his power not to will to stay in the room. Although the action of leaving the room was not available to the agent, his voluntary action of staying was not necessitated. Had he not willed to stay, his voluntary action of staying would not have occurred.

An interesting challenge to the idea that we are morally responsible for our action only if we could have willed to refrain has been advanced by Harry Frankfurt.[5] To see the challenge, consider the following example. Suppose a mad scientist has gained access to your volitional capacity and not only can tell what act of will you are about to bring about but, worse yet, can send electrical currents into your brain that will cause a particular act of will to occur even though it is not the act of will that you would have brought about if left to your own devices. We will suppose that you are deliberating on a matter of great concern: killing Jones. Our mad scientist happens to be interested in Jones's going on to his reward, but he wants Jones to die by your hand. His complicated machinery tells him that you are about to conclude your deliberations by willing *not* to kill Jones. Quickly, he pushes the buttons, sending certain currents into your brain with the result that the volition to kill Jones occurs in you and results, let us say, in your actually killing Jones. Clearly you are not morally accountable here for your act of will and subsequent action of

5. Harry G. Frankfurt, "Alternate Possibilities and Moral Responsibility," *Journal of Philosophy* 66 (1969):829–39.

killing Jones. Were matters left to you, you would have willed not to kill Jones and would not have killed him. Although on Reid's account of this case it would be true that you willed to kill Jones, you were not the agent-cause of your act of will and are therefore not morally accountable for your willing and your action.

Our second case is similar to, but also crucially different from, the first. The mad scientist is intent on seeing to it that Jones is killed by your hand. But rather than activate the machine to cause your act of will to kill Jones, he would prefer that you bring about that act of will and the subsequent action of killing Jones. This time, however, your deliberations result in your act of will to kill Jones. The mad scientist could and would have caused that act of will in you had you been going to will not to kill Jones. But no such action was necessary on his part. There is a process in place (the machine, etc.) that assures that you shall will to kill Jones. But the process is activated *only if* you are not going to will to kill Jones. Given the machine, it was not in your power to avoid willing to kill Jones. But this fact *played no role* in what actually led to your willing to kill Jones and the actual killing that resulted. In this case, we do wish to hold you morally responsible for your act of will and the resulting action. And this is so even though it was not in your power to prevent your willing to kill Jones and not in your power to refrain from killing Jones.

Frankfurt argues that the fact that there are circumstances that make it impossible for an agent to avoid performing a certain action diminishes or extinguishes moral accountability for the action only if those circumstances in some way *bring it about* that the agent performs the action in question. This is true in our first case, where the mad scientist pushes the buttons that send the current causing the agent's volition to kill Jones. Here the circumstances that prevent the agent from *not* willing to kill Jones *bring about* his volition to kill Jones. But in the second case, the circumstances that make it impossible for the agent not to will to kill Jones *play no role* in bringing it about that the agent willed to kill Jones. As Frankfurt remarks: "For those circumstances, by hypothesis, actually had nothing to do with his having done what he did. He would have done precisely the same thing . . . even if they had not prevailed."[6] It is because these circumstances play no role in what the agent willed and did that the agent bears moral responsibility for his volition and act, even though it was not in his power to refrain from doing what he did. I believe Frankfurt is right about this matter. What remains to be seen, however, is whether Reid's basic intuition of a necessary connection between moral accountability and power over the will is unable to accommodate the case in which the agent is morally accountable but cannot prevent willing to kill Jones.

The second mad scientist example shows that an agent may be morally accountable for an act of will to do A even though it is not in the agent's power not to will that action. This certainly appears to conflict with Reid's theory, but we need to recall here that what is *crucial* for Reid's view of moral accountability is that the person be the *agent-cause* of his volition to do A. His view is that the agent is morally accountable for his voluntary action only if he is the agent-cause of his volition to do A. Now we already have seen that he may be the agent-cause of his volition to do A and not have it in his power not to will that action (or to agent-cause the volition to refrain from doing A). This is what we learned, in part, from our second mad scientist case. But here, I believe, we need to distinguish between

1. It was in the agent's power not to will doing A.

and

2. It was in the agent's power *not* to cause his volition to do A.

6. "Alternate Possibilities and Moral Responsibility," 837.

In our second mad scientist case, (1) is false. But (2) is not false. The agent does have the power not to cause his volition to do A. The mad scientist has so arranged matters that the machine automatically causes the volition to do A in our agent if, but only if, the agent is about to not will to do A. This being so, (1) is clearly false. The agent cannot prevent his willing to do A; for if he does not cause his willing to do A, the machine will cause his act of will to do A. But it still may be up to the agent whether *he* shall be the cause of his volition to do A. This power, Reid would argue, depends on a number of factors: the will of God, the continued existence of the agent, the absence of prior internal events and circumstances determining the occurrence of the volition to do A, etc. It also depends on the mad scientist's decision to activate the machine *only if* the agent is about to not will to do A. The scientist can cause our agent to will to do A. He does this by causing that act of will in the agent.[7] But if he does so then the agent does not agent-cause his volition to do A. The real agent-cause is the scientist. So if the agent has the power to cause his volition to do A, he also has the power *not to cause* that volition. If he does not cause the volition and the machine activates, he nevertheless wills to do A—but *he* is not the cause of that act of will. I propose, therefore, the following as representing Reid's basic intuition concerning the connection between moral accountability and power.

> P. A person is morally accountable for his action A only if he causes the volition to do A and it was in his power not to cause his volition to do A.[8]

7. I take Reid to hold (rightly) that causing a volition to do A in an agent is to cause *the agent's willing to do A*. Thus, when an agent wills to do A, we can raise the question of whether the cause of his so willing is the agent himself or something else.

8. As noted in the previous chapter, we do hold persons accountable for actions that they do not will. But we may take Reid's account of freedom as what is entailed by those *voluntary* actions for which we are morally responsible.

(I believe this principle expresses Reid's view of our moral accountability for volitions as well. Simply replace 'action A' with 'volition to do A.')

Principle P accords with our intuitions concerning both of the mad scientist cases. In the first case, when the machinery causes the volition to do A, we do not wish to hold the agent morally accountable for the volition and its causal products. After all, if left to himself he would have willed to refrain from doing A. In the second case, where the machinery is not activated, we do hold the agent responsible for the volition and the action of killing Jones. And this is just what principle P will support. For the agent caused his volition to kill Jones and had it in his power not to cause that volition. I suggest, therefore, that the Frankfurt examples do not refute the thesis that moral responsibility for a voluntary action implies Reidian freedom with respect to that action.

It might be suggested that a supersophisticated scientist could so arrange his machine that if the agent were about not to cause his volition to do A the machine would activate, causing him to *cause* his volition to do A. If so, and if our agent does cause his volition, with the result that the machine is not activated, isn't our agent responsible even though it is not in his power *not to cause* his volition? The Reidian reply to this is that it is *conceptually impossible* to cause an *agent* to cause (in Reid's sense) his volition. For, as we've earlier noted, an agent has active power to cause only if he has power not to cause. This claim is a conceptual truth for Reid. "Power to produce any effect, implies power not to produce it" (523).

We've seen that on Reid's account the core of the libertarian doctrine is that we sometimes have power over the determinations of our will, power to cause or not to cause certain acts of will (volitions). To fully understand his theory of freedom, however, we need to examine his account of acts of will (volitions), see how they are distinguished from other mental states or acts, consider their relations to various sorts of human action, and try to determine the extent to which Reid believes we possess such a power over the determinations of our will.

A volition is an act of the mind, a determination of the mind or will to do or not do something. A volition, then, may have as its object the doing of an action or the refraining from the doing of an action. Like remembering, thinking, and desiring, willing, on Reid's account, is an intentional act; it must have an object. Unlike these other mental acts, which also take an object, willing takes only *our own action* as its object. We may, for example, desire the happiness of our children (which is not an action) or desire that they behave well (which is not our own action). Indeed, with respect to our own action, Reid notes that we may desire what we do not will and will what we do not desire.

> A judge, from a regard to justice, and to the duty of his office, dooms a criminal to die, while, from humanity or particular affection, he desires that he should live. A man, for health, may take a nauseous draught, for which he has no desire, but a great aversion. Desire, therefore, even when its object is some action of our own, is only an incitement to will, but it is not volition. The determination of the mind may be, not to do what we desire to do. But, as desire is often accompanied by will, we are apt to overlook the distinction between them. (532)

Reid makes two points in connection with the fact that an act of will always has one's own action as its object. The first is that in order for a person to will the doing (refraining) of a certain action the person "must have some conception, more or less distinct, of what he wills" (531). I cannot will to deduce Bayes's Theorem from the axioms of the probability calculus unless I have some conception of Bayes's Theorem, the axioms, and the deductive process. An immediate consequence of this point is that infants lack free will. They lack free will because they are unable to engage in acts of will, lacking a conception of what it is that they do. "A healthy child, some hours after its birth, feels the sensation of hunger, and, if applied to the breast, sucks and swallows its food very perfectly. We have no reason to think, that, before it ever sucked, it has any conception of that complex operation, or how it is performed. It cannot, therefore, with propriety, be said that it wills to suck" (531). Reid's second point is that the action willed "must be something which we believe to be in our power, and to depend upon our will" (532). This is an interesting restriction on our power over the determinations of our will. We have no power to cause a volition to do action A unless we believe action A to be within our power. As Reid remarks: "A man may desire to make a visit to the moon, or to the planet Jupiter, but he cannot will or determine to do it: because he knows it is not in his power" (532). Reid acknowledges that persons appear to will to do certain actions when they may be doubtful that the actions lie within their power. In such cases, Reid suggests that what the person wills is *to try* to do the action (532).

Before considering Reid's other remarks about volition, it is helpful here to note a significant disparity between Reid and Clarke on the question of the extent of liberty. Clarke holds that the power to act or not act is coextensive with living beings. Every living thing is essentially free; it has power over its actions. None of its actions can be causally necessitated. In response to Collins's assumption that the advocates of free will allow that children and beasts act of necessity, Clarke responds:

> The actions of children, and the actions of every living creature, are all of them essentially free. The mechanical and involuntary motions of their bodies, such as the pulsation of the heart, and the like, are indeed all necessary; but they are none of them actions. Every action, every motion arising from the self-moving principle, is essentially free. The difference is this only. In men, this physical liberty is joined with a sense or consciousness of moral good and evil, and is therefore eminently called liberty. In beasts, the same physical liberty or self-moving

> power, is wholly separate from a sense or consciousness or capacity of judging of moral good and evil; and is vulgarly called spontaneity. In children, the same physical liberty always is from the very beginning; and in proportion as they increase in age, and in capacity of judging, they grow continually in degree, not more free, but more moral agents.[9]

In Chapter 2 we saw that Clarke identifies being free with "having a continual power of choosing, whether he shall act, or whether he shall forbear acting." When we combine this view with the passage just quoted, we begin to see a substantial difference between his view of the range of freedom and Reid's. Both see freedom as essentially a matter of power over the determinations of the will, a power of choosing or not choosing. But Clarke sees this power as unlimited by a being's ability to understand what is being willed and unlimited by a being's beliefs concerning what it can and cannot do. So he has no reluctance to attribute such a power to infants and beasts. Reid, however, in addition to limiting the ascription of acts of will to beings who have a conception of the action willed and a belief that the action lies within their power, is prepared to limit *power* over our volitions to those beings who have a sufficient degree of reason to make *judgments* concerning what actions are wise or foolish, right or wrong.

> We may, perhaps, be able to conceive a being endowed with power over the determinations of his will, without any light in his mind to direct that power to some end. But such power would be given in vain. No exercise of it could be either blamed or approved. As nature gives no power in vain, I see no ground to ascribe a power over the determinations of the will to any being who has no judgment to apply it to the direction of his conduct, no discernment of what he ought or ought not to do. (600)

9. *Works* 4:729.

The implication of all this is that Reid is prepared to allow that a being may have volitions without having free will, without having a power over those volitions. Thus he remarks about animals and about humans before they are able to use reason: "What kind or what degree of liberty belongs to brute animals, or to our own species, before any use of reason, I do not know. We acknowledge that they have not the power of self-government. Such of their actions as may be called *voluntary* seem to be invariably determined by the passion, or appetite, or affection, or habit, which is strongest at the time." (600). In terms of the infant, Reid's view appears to be this. At birth there are "actions" (sucking at the breast, etc.). But these are not *voluntary* actions since they are not willed. The infant cannot will what s/he cannot conceive. And just after birth the infant has not yet developed concepts of such "actions." But, presumably there comes a period when the young child has some conception of certain actions and may be said to will them. We have, therefore, a distinction between actions that are not willed and actions that are voluntary because they are willed. Still, the young child, although understanding to some degree the action, may not have reached that stage in the development of its reason where s/he is capable of exercising *judgment* concerning the actions s/he is capable of conceiving. The young child may still be unable to judge whether the contemplated action is wise or foolish, right or wrong. At this point, Reid is inclined to view the young child as possessing will in the sense of having volitions, but not as possessing *free* will in the sense of having a power to determine the will, a power to cause or not cause a given volition. Such a power Reid thinks would be given in vain. For the individuals would determine their volitions" in the dark, without any reason, motive, or end" (600). "I see no ground to ascribe a power over the determinations of the will to any being who has no judgment to apply it to the direction of his conduct, no discernment of what he ought or ought not to do" (600). What, then, does determine the volitions in beings before they have the capacity to judge whether their contemplated actions be wise or foolish, right or wrong? Reid's answer is that they are determined by passion, appetite, affection, or habit, whichever is the strongest at the time. Moreover, when humans do reach the point of rational judgment, their power over the determinations of their wills remains a fragile thing. In the delirium of fever or a state of madness, humans lose the capacity for rational judgment. Their wills are determined by the strongest nonrational factors. And even when reason makes its judgments in terms of what is right or best in the long run, our passions may be so inflamed as to overcome our power to will in accordance with reason. So, far from Clarke, who views humans and animals as possessing always a power to choose to act or not act, Reid sees this power as altogether absent when a being lacks an understanding of the "actions" performed; as largely absent (or at least without purpose) when a being lacks judgment as to the wisdom or foolishness, rightness or wrongness of the action under consideration; and subject to being overcome when the passions become greatly inflamed. Indeed, in contrast to Clarke, it is clear that Reid has little interest in *liberty per se,* a power over the determinations of the will. His concern is *moral liberty,* a power over the determinations of the will in a person who has sufficient practical reason to form judgments about what in conduct is right or wrong, wise or foolish. It is, he thinks, conceivable for a creature without practical judgment to possess active power. But such a power would be given in vain. "as reason without active power can do nothing, so active power without reason has no guide to direct it to any end" (615).

Reid's final remark about the will as a power to cause or not cause various volitions is that this power would be of no use whatever unless in all important determinations to act or not act there is "something in the preceding state of the mind that disposes or inclines us to that determination" (533). If there were no such something, then whenever we are confronted with a choice to act or not act we should either not will to act at all or our volitions would be random and meaningless, neither wise nor foolish, neither virtuous nor vicious. In fact, however, there are a variety of *principles of action* that incite or provide motivation for our volitions, and one of the tasks we must address in a later chapter is to determine what these principles of action are and how it is that they may influence what volitions occur in us without robbing us of free will. For the moment it suffices to note that Reid divides up the principles of actions into three sorts: mechanical principles, animal principles, and rational principles. The first (mechanical) include *instinct* and *habit* and normally operate without any volitions, as, for example, when by instinct the infant sucks at the breast or an adult responds immediately to correct his balance after stumbling. The second (animal) include *appetite, affections,* and *passions* and normally operate by influencing volitions but do not involve judgments concerning the wisdom or moral worth of the action contemplated. The final (rational) necessarily involve judgment concerning what is right or wrong, wise or foolish.

Reid's chief interest is to distinguish the different ways in which the rational and animal principles influence the will. The distinction is not just one of degree but also of kind. It is this difference in the ways of influence that bears directly on the issue of free will. We will return to it later. It suffices here to quote Reid's most succinct statement of the difference.

> It is one thing to push a man from one part of the room to another; it is a thing of a very different nature to use arguments to persuade him to leave his place and go to another. He may yield to the force which pushes him, without any exercise of his rational faculties; nay, he must yield to it, if he do not oppose an equal or a greater force. His liberty is impaired in some degree; and, if he has not power sufficient to oppose, his liberty is quite taken away, and the motion cannot be imputed to him at all. The influence of appetite or passion seems to me to be very like this. If the passion be supposed irresistible, we impute the action to it solely, and not to the man. If he had power to resist,

but yields after a struggle, we impute the action partly to the man, and partly to the passion.

If we attend to the other case, when the man is only urged by arguments to leave his place, this resembles the operation of the cool or rational principle. It is evident that, whether he yields to the arguments or not, the determination is wholly his own act, and is entirely to be imputed to him. Arguments, whatever be the degree of their strength, diminish not a man's liberty; they may produce a cool conviction of what we ought to do, and they can do no more. But appetite and passion give an impulse to act, and impair liberty, in proportion to their strength. (536)

6

Reid's Arguments for Libertarian Freedom

If it cannot be proved that we always act from necessity, there is no need of arguments on the other side, to convince us that we are free agents.

—Thomas Reid

In Reid's writings several lines of argument are advanced for the view that we possess moral liberty, that we sometimes have power over the determinations of our will. Reid gives separate treatment to three arguments: from the natural belief in free will, from moral accountability, and from the fact that we can carry out plans of conduct. In addition to these three, there is a very interesting argument that appears now and then in *Essays on the Active Powers of Man* but is not set forth as a separate argument for free will. I will begin with a discussion of this last argument.

Necessitarians grant that some of our voluntary actions are in our power, that it is up to us whether they occur. They grant, for example, that it often is in a person's power to walk or refrain from walking. These actions, however, depend on the will. He walks only if he so wills. And he performs the act of refraining from walking only if he wills to refrain. Which action he performs depends, therefore, on what he wills. But, argues Reid, it is impossible that the action be in the person's power and that upon which the action *depends* be not in his power. Therefore, on some occasions the determinations of the will must be in the person's power.

This argument is worthy of serious consideration. It can be set forth as follows:

1. Certain actions are in our power.
2. Bringing about these actions requires that we will them.
therefore,
3. Actions that are in our power depend upon the determinations of our will.
4. If actions that are in our power depend upon the determinations of our will, then the determinations of our will are sometimes in our power.
therefore,
5. The determinations of our will are sometimes in our power.

Perhaps Reid does not give separate treatment to this argument because it begins with the premise that certain actions are in our power. The premise might be conceptually too close to the conclusion to merit treatment as an independent argument for free will. In fact, he appears to use the argument to try to establish an *inconsistency* in the necessitarian position (602). For the necessitarian insists that external actions that depend on our will are within our power. Reid agrees but then argues that it logically follows that we must have power over our wills. Since there is general agreement on the first premise of this argument, it is altogether reasonable to view the argument as an attempt to provide support for free will.

There is little in this argument with which Reid's opponent can disagree. Hobbes, Locke, Collins, etc., assent to (1) and (2). Indeed, for them to deny (1) would be to deny freedom altogether, something the necessitarians were loath to do. (2) simply records the volitional theory of action that is common to both sides in the eighteenth-century debate over liberty and necessity. Actions that are in our power to perform or not to perform cannot occur without our willing them. This leaves us with (4). Reid states the principle from which (4) is derived as follows: "For to say that what depends upon the will is in a man's power, but the will is not in his power, is to say that the end is in his power, but the means necessary to that end are not in his power, which is a contradiction" (602). Since the success of his argument rests on this principle, we had best look at it with some care.

In his perceptive discussion of Reid's view of moral agency and active power, Timothy Duggan argues that Reid must be distinguishing between *necessary means* relative to an end and *necessary conditions* relative to an end. For apart from such a distinction, Duggan notes that his principle collapses. There are many conditions necessary for my achieving a certain end that is in my power, conditions that do not fall within my power. For example, it is in my power to read Moore's *Principia Ethica* this evening. A necessary condition of my doing so is that Moore wrote *Principia Ethica*. But it is not in my power to bring it about that Moore wrote *Principia Ethica*.[1] In the case just mentioned, the condition is logically necessary for my performing the act in question (reading Moore's *Principia Ethica*). It is causally, but not logically, necessary that oxygen be present if I am to run a mile at noon. It is within my power to run a mile at noon. But it is not in my power to bring it about that oxygen is present in the atmosphere at noon. So if Reid is talking about *necessary conditions* his principle is false. Duggan suggests that what Reid means (or should mean) by *necessary means* are "things an agent *does* (or might do) in bringing about some end the agent desires."[2] "Thus, in cer-

1. If p is in my power, and p entails q, it doesn't follow that q is in my power, as the example in the text shows. But the following, I believe, is a correct principle. If p is in my power, p entails q, and q does not obtain, then it is in my power to bring it about that q obtains.

2. "Active Power and the Liberty of Moral Agents," *Thomas Reid: Critical Interpretations*, ed. Stephen F. Barker and Tom L. Beauchamp (Philadelphia: Philosophical Monographs, 1976), 107.

tain circumstances, *sawing* (something an agent does) is a necessary means to the plank's being cut to a particular length. That a saw is available is a necessary condition of the plank's being thus cut. It is not a necessary means."[3] Since an action that *is* in our power may have a necessary causal or logical condition that is not in our power, if such conditions are meant by "necessary means," Reid's principle is false. "If, however, we understand 'necessary means' in the way I suggest—as something the agent does (or might do) which is causally necessary for bringing about the end he desires—then Reid's argument is very persuasive."[4] I think Duggan is pointing us in the right direction. But his suggestion goes wrong in two ways. First, since Reid acknowledges that actions may be involuntary and beyond our power, it can happen that one of my *actions* that is not in my power is a causally necessary condition of some desired end that is in my power. This can be so when there are two actions I must perform such that each is causally necessary and their conjunction causally sufficient for a desired end. The first action may not be in my power; it may be necessitated by prior internal or external events. The end, however, will still be in my power if the second action is in my power. Thus, a mad scientist might so interfere with happenings in my brain as to necessitate my action of loading the rifle and pointing it at Jones. This necessitated action may be causally necessary for my end of killing Jones. But that end still will be in my power provided the action of pulling the trigger remains in my power.

The second defect in Duggan's proposal is that it limits Reid's *necessary means* to actions. It is clear that Reid drew no such limit. Thus in discussing the necessitarian view that there can be no action without a motive, he remarks: "If a man could not act without a motive, he would have no power at all; for motives are not in our power; and he that has not

3. "Active Power and the Liberty of Moral Agents," 107.
4. "Active Power and the Liberty of Moral Agents," 107.

power over a necessary mean, has not power over the end" (609). If Reid limited necessary means to actions, this passage would make no sense. Clearly, he is arguing that if the motive that gives rise to the action were necessary for the action, then the motive would be a necessary means of the action. The action, however, is in our power and motives are not. So, by the principle that an end can be in our power only if the necessary means to it are in our power, Reid concludes that motives cannot be necessary for actions.

Duggan's point remains, however, that some distinction must be drawn between a necessary means of an action and a necessary condition of an action. For actions may be in our power while their necessary conditions that obtain are not. Suppose a spigot's being in the "on" position will result in the liquid flowing out of the vat. Moreover, if the spigot is not in the "on" position, the liquid will not flow out of the vat. Suppose, finally, that it is in my power to determine whether or not the liquid flows from the vat. In this case, it must be in my power to determine whether or not the spigot occupies the "on" position. Here, I believe, we have a genuine case of a *necessary means* relative to the end of the liquid flowing from the vat. The spigot's being on is a *necessary* condition of the liquid's flowing from the vat, and it is a *means* by which the end is attained. Since it is a means to the end and is necessary to the end, it is a necessary means to the end. And what Reid claims is true: the end is in my power only if the necessary means to that end is also in my power. If I do not have power over the spigot's position (on or not on), then I do not have power over whether the liquid remains or flows out of the vat.

My point is that a condition may be necessary for an end without being a means to that end, without being something that in the circumstances brings about the end. Oxygen being present is a necessary condition but not a means to my running a mile at noon. A means to an end is a condition or event such that its obtaining in the circumstances that prevail is sufficient for realizing the end. So if the end doesn't obtain, the means doesn't obtain. Of course, there may be several distinct means to the same end. If so, I need not have power over each of the means in order to have power over the end. In addition to the spigot being in the "on" position, it could be that there is a plug in the vat that when pulled will result in the liquid flowing from the vat. In that case the spigot's being in the "on" position is a means but not a necessary means relative to the end of the liquid flowing from the vat. But if a means is *necessary* for attaining the end, then I must have power over that means if I am to have power over the end.

Necessitarians believe that the (strongest) motive is a means to the action that results. Reid's point is that if such a motive were also necessary, it would follow that the action is not in our power—for motives are not in our power. Duggan objects to this argument on the grounds that Reid himself admits that there is a sense of 'deliberate action' such that motives are necessary for the occurrence of these actions. But Reid, I believe, would not himself adopt the necessitarian view that the (strongest) motive is a means in the sense of something sufficient for the action that follows. For on his view, as opposed to the necessitarian's view, motives are never causally sufficient for *free* actions. It is always in the power of the agent not to will the action. And when it is not in the power of the agent not to will the action—when the motive is irresistible—the end in question (the action) is not in the agent's power, for it is not a free action.

Actions that are free in the necessitarian sense are such that the appropriate act of will is a necessary means to their occurrence. For on the necessitarian view, a free action is one that wants *only* the appropriate act of will for its occurrence. The other conditions necessary for the action—conditions having to do with ability and opportunity—are either already present or will be supplied should the act of will occur. The necessitarian also agrees with Reid that the appropriate act of will is necessary for the occurrence of the free section. Hence, the appropriate act of will is a necessary means of the free action that results from it. But if so, then the action is in our power only if the appropriate act of will is in our power. Since the necessitarian holds that free actions are in our power, but the necessary means of those actions (the appropriate acts of will) are not in our power, the necessitarian position is contradictory.

As persuasive as Reid's argument is, I believe it is unsuccessful against the necessitarian position. At most, the argument shows that there is a sense of 'in our power' such that our actions are in our power (in that sense) only if the determinations of our will on which the actions depend are in our power. But for the argument to be effective against the necessitarian, it must establish that the *necessitarian's sense* of 'in our power' is such that our actions are in our power (in that sense) only if the acts of will on which those actions depend are in our power (in that sense or some other relevant sense). To determine the latter we must set forth what the necessitarian means when he asserts that certain actions are in our power. Once that is settled, we can then determine whether Reid's principle that the end is in our power only if the necessary means is in our power is true when 'in our power' is used in the necessitarian's sense.

What does the necessitarian mean when he says that it was in the agent's power to do action A? What he means (roughly) is that at the time in question there existed a set of conditions necessary for the agent's doing A such that the agent's then willing to do A would have resulted in a set of conditions sufficient for the agent's doing A. If some condition necessary for the agent's doing A was absent at the time and *would not have obtained* even if the agent had willed to do A, then clearly it is not true that it was in the agent's power to do A. Roughly, then, we can express the necessitarian account of

1. It was in the agent's power to do A.

as follows:

2. There existed a set of conditions necessary for the agent's doing A such that had the agent willed to do A there would have existed a set of conditions sufficient for the agent's doing A.

As we've seen, there are forceful objections to the view that (1) is logically equivalent to (2). First, although (2) seems to follow from (1), it does not appear to imply (1). For, as the free will advocates would argue, in addition to (2) it must also be true that the agent had it in his power to *will* to do A. Second, there is the problem that (2) may be true because of some unusual factors, factors making for "lucky success." From the fact that someone would have done A had he willed to do A, it does not follow that it was in his power to have done A. For his success might have been merely lucky, due to unusual factors quite beyond the agent's control. But whatever objections there may be to the necessitarian's account of (1) in terms of (2), the issue here is not these objections but whether Reid's argument successfully shows that the necessitarian is committed to allowing that the acts of will, which are the necessary means to actions of which (2) is true, must be in our power. And I think a moment's reflection is sufficient to show that his argument cannot successfully show this. For it is obvious, I believe, that the truth of (2) does not require the truth of (3).

3. It was in the agent's power to will to do A.

The truth of (2) requires *only* that circumstances were such that had the agent willed to do A he would have done A. Clearly, circumstances could have been as required for the agent's willing to have resulted in his doing A *even* if the agent did not have power over the determinations of his will. It may be that given the agent's desires, etc., it was causally impossible for the agent to will to do A. It hardly follows from this supposition that (2) is false. So (2) does not require (3). And if we take (2) as what the necessitarian means by (1), we must conclude that, so understood, (1) does not require the truth of (3).

If the above is correct, where does Reid's argument go astray? It goes astray in statement (4) and in the principle from which (4) is derived. According to (4), if an action that is in our power depends upon the determination of our will, then the determination of our will is in our power. As we've seen, however, this claim is false when it expresses the necessitarian's sense of 'in our power.' Actions may be in our power in the necessitarian's sense even though the acts of will on which they depend are not in our power.[5] What of Reid's general principle from which (4) is derived? His principle, I believe, comes to this: If I have power over whether X occurs, and Y is necessary and sufficient (in the circumstances) for X to occur, then I must have power over whether Y occurs. There are senses of 'in our power' for which this principle is correct. It fails, however, when an action that is in our power (in the necessitarian's sense) is substituted for X, and an act of will on which that action depends is substituted for Y. For, as we've seen, action A was in my power just in case my willing to do A was necessary and would have been sufficient for the occurrence of A. But the truth of the latter does not require that willing A was in my power. Reid's argument, therefore, fails to establish an inconsistency in the necessitarian's position.

As we noted at the outset, Reid gives separate treatment to three arguments for the conclusion that we possess moral liberty. Of these three, the first two (from the natural belief in free will; from moral accountability) play a central role in his thinking and are clearly worthy of serious consideration. His

5. In the necessitarian's sense of 'in our power,' acts of will are not the sort of things that can be in our power. According to the necessitarians, acts of will are the causal products of desires, judgments, and the like. They are not the result of acts of will that have *them* for their objects.

third argument (from the fact that we can carry out plans of conduct) is, I believe, less impressive and will be passed over in what follows.[6]

Reid's first argument "to prove that man is endowed with moral liberty" is "because he has a natural conviction or belief, that, in many cases, he acts freely" (616). He states the argument more fully in the first paragraph of the chapter devoted to it:

> *We have, by our constitution a natural conviction or belief, that we act freely*—a conviction so early, so universal, and so necessary in most of our rational operations, that it must be the result of our constitution, and the work of Him that made us. (616)

Having (apparently) stated his first argument for the reality of moral liberty, Reid notes that some necessitarians admit to the existence of such a natural conviction but conclude that it is delusive.[7] He then argues that such a view is dishonorable to "our Maker." For it implies that God so constituted us as to naturally produce a false belief. Indeed, since the irresistible beliefs produced by our constitution are, in a way, the "voice of God" to us, the necessitarian view that this irresistible belief is false "imputes a lie to the God of truth" (617). Finding this position "shocking," Reid dismisses it and proceeds in the bulk of the chapter to produce the evidence in support of his claim that we do have a natural conviction that we sometimes act freely.

The problem in understanding this argument for human freedom is to supply the missing premise. For the main burden of the chapter devoted to the argument is to prove that we have a natural belief whose content is that we sometimes

6. The argument from the fact that we can carry out plans of conduct is examined and criticized by Duggan in "Active Power and Moral Agents."

7. In his notes to Reid's text, Hamilton mentions Lord Kames and several other necessitarians as illustrations of Reid's point.

act freely. Suppose we grant this point to Reid. How do we then get to the conclusion that we sometimes act freely, that the belief in question *is true?*

It may be that the missing premise is simply that irresistible beliefs that arise from our constitution are true. Alternatively, as suggested by Reid's remarks about God, the missing premise may be that irresistible beliefs that arise from our constitution are due to "our maker" and therefore must be true.

Perhaps, however, Reid is not really doing what he says he is doing: giving a proof of the reality of freedom. Perhaps he is trying to expose the necessitarian as having inconsistent beliefs. For just as the skeptic cannot but believe that there are trees, houses, and other human beings, despite his skepticism, so the necessitarians are bound to believe themselves to sometimes act freely, despite their speculative doctrine that, as Collins put it, "a power to act or not to act, to do this or another thing under the same causes, is an impossibility."

Finally, we should note a possibility suggested by Reid's remark in concluding the chapter.

> This natural conviction of our acting freely, which is acknowledged by many who hold the doctrine of necessity, ought to throw the whole burden of proof upon that side; . . . If it cannot be proved that we always act from necessity, there is no need of arguments on the other side to convince us that we are free agents.
>
> To illustrate this by a similar case:—if a philosopher would persuade me that my fellow-men with whom I converse are not thinking, intelligent beings, but mere machines, though I might be at a loss to find arguments against this strange opinion, I should think it reasonable to hold the belief which nature gave me before I was capable of weighing evidence, until convincing proof is brought against it. (620)

We have, then, at least three different ways of construing the argument based on our having a *natural belief* that we act freely, only the first of which would result in a valid argument for the reality of human freedom. The first way adds as the second premise either

2a. Natural beliefs that arise from our constitution are true.

or

2b. Natural beliefs that arise from our constitution are due to God (who would be a deceiver were such beliefs false).

The second way construes the argument as establishing an inconsistency in the necessitarian position. To do so all that need be shown is that in spite of denying the truth of the belief that we are sometimes free, the necessitarian is himself committed to the belief. Apart from whether he shows this to be so, it is clear that Reid affirms it:

> There are some points of belief so necessary, that, without them, a man would not be the being which God made him. These may be opposed in speculation, but it is impossible to root them out. In a speculative hour they seem to vanish, but in practice they resume their authority. This seems to be the case of those who hold the doctrine of necessity, and yet act as if they were free. (619)

Finally, we may construe the argument as establishing not the *truth* of the belief that we are free but the *epistemic right* to believe that we are free. Accordingly, the second premise of this third way of construing Reid's argument would be something like:

2c. Natural beliefs that arise from our constitution are such that it is reasonable to believe them true until we have convincing proofs of their falsity.

It is at the very least relevant to our problem of how to understand Reid's argument to note that its initially announced conclusion (that we sometimes act freely) is regarded by Reid as a first principle of common sense, one of those principles that is believed merely on being understood, that neither requires nor admits of proof, and is the irresistible product of our constitution. Thus in his *Essays on the Intellectual Powers of Man,* Reid's sixth instance of the first principles of contingent truths is: "That we have some degree of power over our actions, and the determinations of our will" (446). The evidence he offers to show that this principle meets the criteria of "First Principles" duplicates the points he makes (in his *Essays on the Active Powers of Man*) in support of the view that the belief that we act freely is the result of our constitution.[8] He mentions, for example, our *acts of will* to perform certain actions, our *acts of deliberation* concerning whether to perform certain actions, and our *resolutions* with regard to performing certain actions. All these operations of the mind imply a belief that the actions in question are within our power, that we have some degree of active power. This being so, Reid concludes that the belief in question must be as universal among human beings and as necessary to their conduct as are the fundamental operations of willing, deliberating, resolving, etc. "We cannot recollect by memory when it [the belief] began. It cannot be a prejudice of education, or of false philosophy. It must be a part of our constitution, or the necessary result of our constitution and therefore the work of God" (618).

Given (1), that Reid expressly says that he is giving an argument for the reality of human freedom, and (2) that the proposition that we sometimes act freely (that we have some degree of active power) is held by him to be one of the fundamental principles of common sense, I think the most

8. The belief that we act freely is equivalent for Reid to the belief that we have some degree of active power, or power over our actions. Within a page of mentioning our "natural conviction or belief that we act freely," he says: "let us proceed to consider the evidence of our having a natural conviction that we have some degree of active power" (617).

plausible of the three ways of understanding his argument is the first. Of the two different alternatives for the second premise, 2a and 2b, I suggest 2a: Natural beliefs that arise from our constitution are true. The reason for preferring 2a to 2b (Natural beliefs that arise from our constitution are due to God) is simply that Reid thinks our knowledge of the existence of God is derived from the fundamental principles of common sense. So, unless the natural beliefs arising from our constitution are themselves justified, we would not be justified in believing the existence of God. It would be therefore circular to appeal to the existence of God as rational support for the truth of the natural beliefs arising from our constitution.[9]

As I've filled out Reid's argument, it is roughly equivalent to the claim that our belief that we sometimes have power to act or not act is a fundamental principle of common sense, that the fundamental principles of common sense are true, and that therefore it is true that we sometimes have power over our actions. Undoubtedly, this argument rightly deserves "first place" in the battery of arguments that Reid would view as supportive of libertarianism. As a direct argument for his view it is, I believe, both important and of genuine merit. Against it, the necessitarian has three countermoves. First, he may argue that the belief that we sometimes have power to act or not act is simply the belief that we sometimes possess power to act (not act) *if so acting (not acting) is what we will.* Anticipating this move, Reid has a response prepared. Before we look at the response, however, we need to note a special point Reid makes in connection with promising.

In addition to claiming that certain operations of the mind (willing to perform some action, deliberating about whether to perform some action, resolving to perform a certain action)

9. Reid suggests that Descartes begs the question in trying to justify that his faculties are not fallacious by using them to prove the existence of a being (God) who would not allow our faculties to be fallacious (447).

require that the agent believe the action in question to be in his power, Reid also claims that *promising* to do something requires that we believe it in our power to do that thing—at least, if the promise is sincerely made. But about promising Reid makes a further point. "There is a condition implied in every promise, *if we live* and *if God continue with us the power which he hath given us*" (617). His point, I take it, is that when we make a promise we incur an *obligation* to do what we have promised to do. But there are certain conditions, more or less understood, which, if not fulfilled, relieve us of the obligation incurred by the promise. (I assume these conditions do not have a similar relation to willing, deliberating, and resolving.)

We can now consider Reid's rejoinder to the necessitarian's first move.

> If we act upon the system of necessity, there must be another condition implied in all deliberation, in every resolution, and in every promise; and that is, *if we shall be willing*. But the will not being in our power, we cannot engage for it. (617)

The conclusion Reid draws is that on the system of necessity "there can be no deliberation, or resolution, nor any obligation in a promise. A man might as well deliberate, resolve, and promise, upon the actions of other men as upon his own" (617–18).

Suppose you are deliberating about mowing the lawn this afternoon. According to Reid, your deliberation is impossible unless you *believe* that it is up to you whether you do or don't mow the lawn this afternoon, that it is in your power to mow the lawn and in your power to refrain from mowing the lawn. On the system of necessity, however, what you believe is that it is in your power to mow it (refrain from mowing it) if that should be what you will. Moreover, whether you shall will to mow or not mow is something that is not in your power. For according to the system of necessity the will is determined by antecedent causes such that, given the causes, there can be no power to will or not will. Suppose, then, you understand all this. You understand, that is, (1) that your having power to mow depends on what your will is and (2) that your will is determined by events over which you have no control. If so, then deliberation about whether to mow or not is pointless, if not impossible.

This response by Reid does not, I believe, rest on the principle that having power over the end requires having power over the means. As we earlier saw, this principle is not true when we give the necessitarian reading of 'power over the end.' Reid's response here is that *deliberation* about whether or not to do X requires that we believe that doing X (not doing X) is in our power. If the belief that doing X is in our power is taken to be the belief that doing X is in our power provided Y obtains, then, once this is understood, deliberation will require that we believe that Y's obtaining is in our power. Once it is clear that Y's obtaining is not in our power, deliberation is pointless, if not impossible.

Suppose I promise you that I will mow the lawn tomorrow. According to Reid, if the promise is sincere I must believe that it is in my power to mow the lawn tomorrow, and I incur an obligation to do what I promise. But on the necessitarian system, my carrying out my promise depends on my willing to mow the lawn, something that must occur if it is necessitated and cannot occur if it is not. Promising, too, becomes pointless, if not impossible.

The necessitarian's second move is to deny that the belief that we have some degree of active power is a fundamental belief of common sense. His third move is to allow that it is, but to require some justification for thinking that such beliefs are *true*. Concerning the former, Reid argues that if such basic operations of the mind as willing, deliberating, and resolving imply the belief in question (as he insists they do), that is sufficient evidence to show that the belief must have its origin in our constitution and that it is natural to us—two marks of fundamental beliefs of common sense. The third move creates more of a difficulty. For a fundamental belief of common sense does not admit of proof. Speaking of another fundamental belief of common sense Reid remarks: "If any man asks a proof of this, I confess I can give him none; there is an evidence in the proposition itself which I am unable to resist" (443). Fundamental beliefs of common sense are universally accepted, irresistible, incapable of practical doubt, the result of our constitution. But need they be true? As opposed to propositions, which we accept on the evidence of other propositions, they are self-evident. But for a proposition to be self-evident it need only be such that upon understanding it the mind believes it to be true. What, then, finally can be said to support the crucial premise in Reid's first argument for freedom: the premise asserting that the fundamental principles of common sense are true? I think the best that can be done—and all that needs to be done—is to justify accepting first principles as true by arguing that we are justified in believing them true until we have some good reason to think them false. Ultimately, this is an appeal to the "authority" of common sense. But it is not a blind appeal to such authority. Reid himself raises the objection: "What has authority to do in matters of opinion? Is truth to be determined by most votes?" (439). Clearly the mere fact that belief is universal and the result of nature, as opposed to education, false philosophy, or whatnot, is no *guarantee* of its truth.

> [But] there must be a great presumption that the judgment of mankind, in such a matter, is the natural issue of those faculties which God hath given them. Such a judgment can be erroneous only when there is some cause of the error, as general as the error is. When this can be shewn to be the case, I acknowledge it ought to have its due weight. But, to suppose a general deviation from truth among mankind in things self-evident, of which no cause can be assigned, is highly unreasonable. (440)

Reid's view, then, is that once it is shown that our belief that we act freely is a fundamental belief of common sense, it follows that we are justified in accepting such a belief as true until it is shown that there is some positive reason to think the belief false. A proof of determinism would be such a reason. But lacking such a proof, we are fully justified in believing the second premise of the argument. Therefore, we are justified in believing that we act freely. With respect to the fundamental beliefs of common sense, we require no further justification for accepting them as true. Only positive evidence against them can overweigh or defeat the prima facie grounds we have for accepting them as true.

Reid's second major argument for the reality of human freedom is perhaps the most commonly used and widely known of the libertarian arguments. The first step in his argument is the claim that we are morally accountable beings, that we are sometimes morally accountable for what we do or refrain from doing. Reid observes that this claim is "proclaimed by every man's conscience" and is one of the principles on which moral systems are grounded. But what follows from the principle that we are sometimes morally accountable for what we do (fail to do)? After noting that the proposition implies some degree of understanding of what we are obligated to do, Reid comes to the second step in his argument.

> Another thing implied in the notion of a moral and accountable being, is *power to do what he is accountable for.* That no man can be under a moral obligation to do what it is impossible for him to do, or to forbear what it is impossible for him to forbear, is an axiom as self-evident as any in mathematics. It cannot be contradicted, without overturning all notion of moral obligation; or can there be an exception to it, when it is rightly understood. (621)

Reid's argument, I believe, proceeds as follows. We are morally accountable beings. To be a morally accountable being is to be such that sometimes one has a moral obligation to do (forbear doing) an action. This is the first step of the argument. The second step is an appeal to the principle that *ought* implies *can.* If a person has a moral obligation to do (forbear doing) an action, then that person has it in his power to do (forbear doing) that action. Therefore, a person sometimes has it in his power to do an action and sometimes has it in his power to forbear doing an action.[10]

Reid thinks that the basic claim (that we are morally accountable beings) on which this argument is based "affords an invincible argument that man is endowed with Moral Liberty" (620). For he thinks that the second premise of his argument is a necessary truth. "*Active power,* therefore, is necessarily implied in the very notion of a morally accountable being" (622). Moreover, although he notes an objection to his second premise, it is clear that he believes that premise to be not only necessary but fairly obviously so. In examining his argument it will be helpful to consider the most common necessitarian response, to examine the objection Reid notes to his second premise, along with his reply, and, finally, to see what modification of his second premise is or may be required by our account in the previous chapter of Reid's conception of human freedom.[11]

The most common necessitarian reply to Reid's argument is to reject Reid's second premise (or to give it an interpretation from which the conclusion of the argument won't follow). According to this view, being morally obligated to do an action requires only that we have power to do the action *if we should will to do it.* But since the necessitarian does not extend to the agent power over the determinations of his will, he cannot agree with Reid that at the time in question the agent

10. As we've seen, on Reid's account of human freedom, once it is established that it is in our power to do a certain action (or in our power to forbear doing an action), it is thereby established that we are sometimes at liberty to do an action (or sometimes at liberty to forbear doing an action).

11. In Chapter 5 I argued that Reid's conception of freedom permits an agent to be morally accountable for doing an action even though it is not in his power to avoid doing it.

must have it in his power to will to do the action. For on the necessitarian account the volition to do A is rendered either causally necessary or causally impossible by factors over which the agent had no control. He can allow that the agent has the *capacity* to have a volition and the *capacity* not to have that volition. But it is one thing to have the capacity to have or not have a volition, as opposed to something like a stone that has no such capacity, and quite another thing to have the active power at the time in question to determine which capacity is to be realized. On Reid's view, if I am morally obligated to do A, then, even though I did not will to do A, it must have been in my power to will to do A. On the necessitarian view, if I did not will to do A, then, given the causes, my willing to do A was causally impossible—in which case, it was not in my power at the time to will to do A.

In denying Reid's second premise, the necessitarian claims that power over the determinations of the will is not necessary for being morally accountable for doing (failing to do) an action. All that is necessary in the way of power—if an agent was morally obligated to perform some action—is that the agent could have done the action if she had willed to do it. But I think this isn't right. For suppose that by stimulating various parts of your brain I can effectively control your volitions. And suppose I thus brought it about that you actively willed to forbear doing that action. Suppose further that, given the circumstances, your willing to forbear doing that action necessitated your not doing that action. Of course, it may still have been true that had you willed to do the action you could have done the action. You were not driven not to do the action *regardless* of what your will might be. But given my activity, you could not will other than to not do the action. Once all this is made clear, isn't it obvious that it is a mistake to suppose that your *moral duty* was to perform the action in question? For in the circumstances there was nothing you could will that would have resulted in your voluntarily performing that action. Since *ought* implies *can* and since you could not do other than will to forbear and thus *not* do the action in question you cannot really have had an obligation to do that action on that occasion. Therefore, you are not morally accountable for that particular failure to act. And since on the system of necessity we never have power over our wills, we will never be morally accountable for doing (forbearing to do) that action. As Reid notes, "accountableness can no more agree with necessity than light with darkness" (616).[12]

Reid notes an objection that has been raised against the axiom that no one can be under a moral obligation to do what is not within his power. The objection is this: "When a man, by his own fault, has disabled himself from doing his duty, his obligation, they say, remains, though he is now unable to discharge it" (621). The objector proposes that we distinguish between the case where some other agent (against your will or knowledge) deprives you of your ability to fulfill your obligation and the case where you willingly and knowingly deprive yourself of your ability to fulfill your obligation. In the former case you would not be morally accountable for failing to do what, without the loss of your ability, you would be obligated to do. But in the latter case, so the objection goes, you continue to be obligated to do what you no longer are able to do. For in the latter case your inability to fulfill your duty is *your own fault.* Thus, to take one of Reid's examples, if a sailor's duty is to climb aloft at his captain's order and if someone should cut off the sailor's fingers, the sailor would cease to be obligated to climb aloft, for it is no longer in his power to do so. But, so the objection goes, if out of desire for the ease of hospital life the sailor cuts off his own fingers, he does not cease to have the obligation to climb aloft at his captain's command—even though it is no longer in his power to fulfill his command. Reid disagrees:

12. The basic point here is that the necessitarian's conception of what it is for an agent to have had the power to do A (could have done A if she had so willed) is inadequate to satisfy the sense of 'can' in *ought* implies *can.*

> He is guilty of a great crime; but after he has been punished according to the demerit of his crime, will his captain insist that he shall still do the study of a sailor? Will he command him to go aloft when it is impossible for him to do it, and punish him as guilty of disobedience? Surely, if there be any such thing as justice and injustice, this would be unjust and wanton cruelty. (621)

Reid's point is that we must distinguish the sailor's duty not to render himself unable to climb aloft from his duty to climb aloft at his captain's command. Once we make this distinction we will see that the sailor's fault and just punishment are connected solely with his violation of his first duty—a violation he presumably could have avoided. But, having cut off his fingers, it is simply mistaken to think that the sailor remains obligated to climb aloft. We may take into account his motive to avoid his duty when we assess his blameworthiness for having cut off his fingers. But once they have been cut off, there can be no obligation any longer for the sailor to climb aloft at his captain's command.[13]

In presenting (in Chapter 5) what I take to be the correct interpretation of Reid's account of free action, I drew certain conclusions from that account with respect to the scope of moral responsibility. Specifically, on the assumption that a free action may be either morally right or morally wrong, I pointed out that a person could be morally accountable for a certain action even though it was not in that person's power to avoid doing the action. For on the interpretation I gave of a Reidian free action, an action is free provided (a) it results from the agent's act of will to perform that action and (b) the agent caused that act of will (having the power not to cause it). Suppose I am deliberating about killing Jones and conclude

13. For some important criticisms of Reid's examples and the claim that *ought* implies *can*, see Keith Lehrer, *Thomas Reid* (London: Routledge and Kegan Paul, 1989), 257–58, 273–76.

my deliberations by agent-causing the volition to kill Jones, with the result that I kill him. On Reid's theory, since it was in my power not to produce that volition ("Power to produce implies power not to produce"), my action was free; I had active power with respect to that action. Suppose, however, that a mechanism exists (a fail-safe cause) that would produce in me the act of will to kill Jones *if but only if* I do not produce it myself. We shall suppose that the volition, regardless of its causal origin (whether me or the mechanism), results in my action of killing Jones. It turns out, then, that my action of killing Jones is unavoidable. For although it is in my power not to cause the act of will to kill Jones, I cannot prevent the occurrence of that volition and the action that flows from it. Moreover, regardless of causal origin, the volition will be *my act of willing*. For it is conceptually impossible for a volition to kill Jones to occur in me without it being true that *I* will to kill Jones.[14] So even if I do not cause the volition to kill Jones, I nevertheless will to kill Jones and perform the action of killing him.

Now killing Jones is an action that, if freely done, is a fit subject for moral evaluation. Since my action was freely done I am morally responsible for it. Thus, given Reid's account of a free action, it turns out that a person may be morally responsible for an action even though the agent couldn't have done otherwise, could not have avoided doing the action. And the question before us is whether this conclusion is consistent with the principle of *ought* implies *can* that constitutes a key premise in Reid's second argument for the reality of human freedom.

My answer is that there is no inconsistency. For an inconsistency arises only if Reid's principle:

> I. An agent is morally obligated to do A (forbear doing A) only if it is in the agent's power to do A (forbear doing A).

14. Willing (like thinking, imagining, and believing) cannot occur in a person without it being true that *the person* wills (thinks, imagines, believes).

is conjoined with a second principle that he does not assert:

> II. If it is morally wrong for an agent to do A (forbear doing A), then the agent is morally obligated to forbear doing A (do A).

For given that it was morally wrong for me to kill Jones, it follows from principle II that I was morally obligated to forbear killing Jones. And given Reid's principle, it then follows that it was in my power to forbear killing Jones, to avoid killing Jones.

What we've seen is that on my interpretation of Reid's account of a free action, if we follow Reid in holding an agent morally responsible for what he does freely, then an agent may be morally responsible for an action even though it was not in his power to avoid doing that action, was not in his power to forebear doing it or to do otherwise. What we've also seen is that this result leads to a contradiction if both principles I and II are adopted. For it will turn out that it both was and was not in my power to avoid killing Jones.[15] Since Reid clearly embraces principle I, we need either to modify my interpretation of Reid's account of a free action or to abandon principle II. Since I think the interpretation has good textual support and since, given principle I, I think we have independent grounds for doubting principle II, I propose that we reject principle II.[16] For quite apart from Reid's theory of freedom, I think our intuitions support the view that I freely kill Jones and am responsible for doing so, even though the existence of the failsafe cause renders me unable to do other-

15. Since Reid would allow that we are morally accountable for our free acts of will (those we cause, having the power not to cause), the same inconsistency would arise when we reformulate principles I and II with respect to volitions.

16. In place of principle II I suggest the following principle: If it is morally wrong for an agent to do A (forbear doing A), then the agent is morally obligated to forbear doing A (do A) if forbearing doing A (doing A) is in his power.

wise. Therefore, if we stick with our intuitions about such cases and accept the fundamental principle that *ought* implies *can,* we really have no alternative but to reject principle II along with the principle of alternate possibilities (If an agent is morally responsible for an action, then he could have done otherwise). This does not mean, however, that the person who does what is morally wrong has no moral obligation not *to cause* his act of will to do that thing.

Because of the fail-safe cause (something that causes my volition *if and only if* I do not), my volition and action may be unavoidable. Suppose, however, that instead of a fail-safe cause there is another being or causal process that simultaneously with me produces my volition and resulting action. If this is possible, my volition to kill Jones could be *overdetermined* and again unavoidable. Is this possible on Reid's theory of what it is to act freely? Could my volition and action be free (in Reid's sense) and also the inevitable causal product of another causal process or agent over which I have no control?

A familiar example of overdetermination is when two light switches turn on the same light. Flipping either switch is causally sufficient for the light going on. If both switches are flipped simultaneously, the event of the light going on is causally overdetermined. The question before us is whether an act of will (and its resulting action) can be overdetermined in the following manner. You as agent cause the occurrence of a particular volition. We will suppose that the volition occurs at t. Perhaps unknown to you some actual causal process, independent of your causal activity, also causes that very same volition to occur at t. If so, then your act of will is causally overdetermined; its occurrence is assured both by the exercise of your power as agent to cause it and by the independent causal process that brings it about at t. Moreover, it appears that we have a further example in which you may be morally accountable for an act of will (and resulting action) that is unavoidable for you. For we will suppose that you exercise no control over the independent causal process that results in the occurrence of your volition at t.

Harry Frankfurt treats the case of overdetermination in the same way that I have treated the case of fail-safe causation. He views it as a genuine counterinstance to the Principle of Alternate Possibilities, the principle that holds that one is morally responsible for an action only if one could have avoided performing it (could have done otherwise). Thus, Frankfurt considers the case of the drug addict who wills to take the drug because that is the desire that he wants to move him all the way to action. On Frankfurt's account, such a person acts freely and of his own free will.[17] But his desire to take the drug is also efficacious because of his physical addiction. The efficaciousness of his first-order desire to take the drug is therefore overdetermined. That desire moves him to action because he wants it to and also because of the force of his physical addiction, either being sufficient to make that desire his will. Suppose, however, that the addiction plays no role in his deliberations. Suppose that had the addiction not been present the addict would still have wanted his first-order desire for the drug to be his will, with the result that that desire would have moved him all the way to action. Given the addiction, the addict could not avoid taking the drug. But, so Frankfurt argues, the fact that he could not do otherwise is here irrelevant to assessing his moral responsibility.

My own view is that the drug addict does not act freely in taking the drug and, accordingly, is not morally responsible for his action. He does not will or act freely because his act of will occurs of necessity. We may say that a volition occurs of

17. Harry G. Frankfurt, "Freedom of the Will and the Concept of a Person," *Journal of Philosophy* 68 (1971):5–20. Although on Frankfurt's view the addict acts freely and of his own free will in taking the drug, he does not have freedom of will, because he is not free to make the first-order desire not to take the drug *his will*. Given his addiction, he is bound to will to take the drug.

necessity when it is the product of an actual causal process over which the agent has no control. Undoubtedly, this would be Reid's own view as well: "if . . . the determination of his will be the necessary consequence of something involuntary in the state of his mind, or of something in his external circumstances, he is not free; he has not what I call the Liberty of a Moral Agent, but is subject to Necessity" (599).[18] Perhaps, then, we should amend Reid's account of what it is to act freely. We can say that an agent acts freely just in case the act of will involved in the action is caused by the agent and is not the causal result of an actual causal process outside the agent's control. In the case of the fail-safe cause, the act of will, when produced by the agent, does not occur of necessity, for there is no actual causal process outside the agent's control that results in the volition.[19]

In this chapter we've looked at three arguments Reid uses to support the factual claim that we sometimes will and act freely. I've criticized his first argument for employing a principle (If the end is in our power then the necessary means for that end must also be in our power) that, although surely true when 'power' is used in Reid's unconditioned sense, is not true when 'power' is used in the necessitarian's conditional sense. The criticism is simply that his argument begs the question against the necessitarian. Hence, his argument fails to establish that the necessitarian is inconsistent in holding both that actions, but not volitions, are in our power and that actions that are in our power depend on the determinations of our will. Concerning his two major arguments (from the natural conviction of active power, from moral accountability) I've had little to say by way of direct criticism. The merit of his first argument de-

18. What is less clear is how Reid's theory of agent-causation can preclude the kind of overdetermination envisaged in the drug addict case.

19. In the fail-safe case it is not up to the agent whether his volition will or will not occur, but it is up to the agent whether it will occur freely or not. For more on this matter see my essay "Causing and Being Responsible for What Is Inevitable," *American Philosophical Quarterly* 26 (1989):153–59.

pends on whether Reid is right in holding (1) that our belief that we sometimes possess active power is universal and the natural product of our constitution and (2) that such beliefs (a) are true or (b) should be believed to be true unless we have some very good reason to believe them false. These are large issues that need greater exploration before a full assessment of his first argument can be given. I will only remark here that I think his evidence in support of (1) is persuasive and that in my judgment it is reasonable to regard such beliefs as true unless we have some good reasons to think them false. As should be clear from my discussion of the argument from moral accountability, I think it has genuine merit. Necessitarian accounts of power are simply inadequate to satisfy the requirements of morality. If we do not have power over our determinations to act or forbear action, then our beliefs about our moral accountability are in some way profoundly mistaken.

7

Reid's Moral Theory

> The man who does not, by the light of his own mind, perceive some things in conduct to be right, and others to be wrong, is as incapable of reasoning about morals as a blind man is about colours.
>
> —Thomas Reid

Reid's moral theory is best understood within the context of his view of the principal natural motives for human actions. In the proper sense of 'action,' Reid takes an action to be something the agent does as a result of willing to do it. Since we can will the doing of something only if we have a conception of what it is we will, an action (in the strict and proper sense) presupposes both will and some degree of understanding. But in the broader sense of the term, an action may occur without any act of will at all. For example, the newborn infant sucks at its mother's breast without willing to do so and without any conception of what it is doing. So one way of dividing up the natural motives of human action, "the Principles of Action," is into those that incite actions without will and understanding and those that incite actions (in the proper sense) that involve will and understanding. As we noted earlier, the first class (instinct and habit) Reid calls the Mechanical Principles of Action. Those motives inciting actions (in the proper sense) Reid divides into two further classes. The second class (appetites, desires, affections) he calls Animal Principles of Action. These principles "operate upon the will and intention, but do not suppose any exercise of judgment or reason; and are most of them found in some brute animals, as well as in man" (551). The final class of natural motives Reid calls the Rational Principles of Action. These motives require the exercise of reason in making judgments of ends. His theory of morals is intimately connected with one of the rational principles of action, the regard for duty.

A principle of action is something in us that incites us, or prompts us, to act. Instinct, "a blind impulse to certain actions," is by definition a principle of action. Our desires for power, esteem, and knowledge also count as principles of action; for when it is determined that a certain action is a means to one of these desired objects, we naturally have some tendency to perform that action. The difference between instinct and desire as principles of action comes to this: The desire prompts the will to initiate the action only if the action is viewed as a means to what is desired. In the case of instinct, the impulse is to the action itself, without any need of an act of will or an understanding of the action to be done. "He is led by nature to do these actions without knowing for what end or what he is about" (533).

As we've noted, Reid divides the animal principles of action from the rational on the grounds that, while both involve will and a conception of what is willed, *judgment* is necessarily involved in the rational principles of action but not in the animal. Since he sets forth two distinct principles of action (a regard for what is our good upon the whole; a regard for what is our duty), each should be distinguished from the animal principles of action by some way in which the making of judgments is required, although the way judgment is required for the first rational principle need not be the way judgment is required for the second.

Obtaining the end of some particular desire (for example, the desire for esteem) yields some degree of happiness. But often obtaining a particular good will prevent us from obtaining a greater good; and sometimes the long-range consequences of pursuing and obtaining a good will themselves be on the whole bad, resulting in considerable unhappiness. Because this is so, we are led to reflect on the various goods we desire, making judgments both of the consequences of obtaining these goods and of the consequences of the actions leading to our obtaining those goods. So doing, we come to form "the conception of what is good or ill upon the whole."

> That brute animals have any conception of this good, I see no reason to believe. And it is evident that man cannot have the conception of it, till reason is so far advanced that he can seriously reflect upon the past, and take a prospect of the future part of his existence. It appears, therefore, that the very conception of what is good or ill for us upon the whole, is the offspring of reason, and can be only in beings endowed with reason. And if this conception give rise to any principle of action in man, which he had not before, that principle may very properly be called a rational principle of action. (581)

A principle of action must be a motive to act. To have the conception of what, in the circumstances, is our good upon the whole would not constitute a principle of action unless we were in some way moved to act so as to obtain what we believe to be our good upon the whole. Reid appears to hold that the intrinsic connection between our good, on the one hand, and our happiness, on the other, is sufficient to generate a desire for what we take to be good. "Whatever makes a man more happy or more perfect, is good, and is an object of desire as soon as we are capable of forming the conception of it. The contrary is ill, and is an object of aversion" (580).[1]

1. It would be a mistake to infer from the connection Reid draws between good and happiness that he thinks that happiness is the only ultimate object of desire. There are many things we desire for their own sakes (esteem, power, etc.). Obtaining these objects yields happiness. But were they not desired as ends in themselves we might find no happiness at all in obtaining them. So we should not conclude that they are not desired as ends but only as means to the happiness that comes with obtaining them.

Reid's first rational principle of action, rational self-love, is meant, at least in a wise person, to regulate the animal principles of action. For although the animal principles may yield some satisfaction when their objects are obtained, they are fundamentally "blind desires of some particular object, without any judgment or consideration, whether it be good for us upon the whole, or ill" (581). Hence, a particular appetite or animal desire may draw us one way, while a regard for what, in the circumstances, would be for our greatest good on the whole draws us in a contrary way. In such a conflict it is evident that a wise and prudent person will endeavor to follow the dictate of rational self-love. When we give way to a blind desire, we see that we have acted against our own best interest; we condemn ourselves for allowing passion to overrule the cool judgment of reason. When we act the better part, placing our enlightened self-interest over our appetites and animal desires, we cannot but feel self-approval. Moreover, Reid argues that the person who assiduously follows the principle of rational self-love will be led to the practice of the virtues, both individual and social. For prudence, temperance, and fortitude are dispositions to act which tend to promote our interest upon the whole. As for the social virtues such as justice and benevolence, their connection to enlightened self-interest is less clear. Reid allows that rational self-love cannot itself produce in us feelings of affection or desire for the good of others. But given that we do desire the happiness of others, then, since the obtaining of the desired end provides *us* with happiness, an enlightened interest in our own good should lead us to exercise our benevolent affections, at least when procuring the welfare of others does not conflict with actions that better serve our own good upon the whole.

If rational self-love has such salutary effects in human life, what need have we of another rational principle of action, a disinterested sense of duty? This question is of some importance to Reid, because he thinks both principles tend to agree in the course of conduct a person should follow. Thus he wants to show that a regard for our own good upon the whole needs to be supplemented by a purely moral principle. To this end he argues: "That, although a regard to our good upon the whole, be a rational principle in man, yet if it be supposed the only regulative principle of our conduct, it would be a more uncertain rule, it would give far less perfection to the human character, and far less happiness, than when joined with another rational principle—to wit, a regard to duty" (586). Undoubtedly, it is a good deal easier to determine the extent to which a proposed action would be conducive to one's own greatest happiness than it is to determine its conduciveness to the happiness of all. But many of our actions take place in circumstances where it is rather difficult to make reasoned judgments of their long-range effects upon our own happiness. Moreover, even when it is clear that a given action will yield us greater happiness than any other action in our power, if the happiness is a distant one it is difficult for rational self-love to win out over the clamor of an animal desire for some immediate good. "Men stand in need of a sharper monitor to their duty than a dubious view of distant good" (584). Of course, if a regard for duty is to make up for this defect in the regard for our good upon the whole, it must be clearer (at least sometimes) that an action is our duty than that it is most conducive to our good upon the whole. And a regard for our duty must be an impetus to action that is sometimes stronger than is our desire for a distant good.

Granted that regard for one's own good upon the whole is a superior principle to those constituted by desires for particular objects, Reid argues that although a person who shapes his conduct to serve his good upon the whole deserves our esteem, he can never exhibit the highest form of virtue that merits our highest esteem. For when all is said and done, such a person acts for himself. Even when he does those actions which are his duty, he does them not for the sake of duty but as a means to his own good. Clearly our highest esteem is reserved for the person "who loves virtue, not for her dowry only, but for her own sake" (585).

Finally, Reid argues that the person who has a regard for duty, as well as a regard for his own good, will have a better chance of obtaining happiness than the person who is motivated only by a concern for his own good upon the whole. For if both, from the moral point of view, do what is their duty, the one does it only for the sake of the happiness it yields; whereas he who acts from duty may have not only the happiness that the action leads to but also the happiness that consists in doing what one desires to do (one's duty). "The one labors only for hire, without any love for the work. The other loves the work, and thinks it the most honourable he can be employed in" (586). This argument has merit provided that the course of conduct duty requires is just what is recommended by the regard for our good upon the whole. Reid thinks that in a morally governed universe this will be true. But what if the world is not morally governed, and our duty is not what is for our own good upon the whole? In that case, of course, the person who acts from duty will enjoy less happiness on the whole than he who calculates correctly and acts solely from rational self-love. Reid, however, dismisses the idea that the two rational principles may conflict as imaginary, suggesting a kind of stalemate should such a conflict ever actually occur. "It will be impossible for the man to act so as not to contradict a leading principle of his nature. He must either sacrifice his happiness to virtue, or virtue to happiness; and is reduced to this miserable dilemma, whether it is best to be a fool or a knave" (598). But it is difficult not to conclude that Reid holds a regard for duty as a superior principle to a regard for one's good upon the whole. For, as we've seen, he thinks that to act from duty deserves greater esteem than to act for oneself. And while discussing the question of which ought to yield he says unequivocally that "the disinterested love of virtue is undoubtedly the noblest principle in human nature, and ought never to stoop to any other" (598).

As we've noted, Reid's second rational principle of action is a regard for what is our duty. As opposed to our conception of what is our good upon the whole, it does not seem that reason must be exercised in making judgments concerning consequences (or other matters) in order to form the conception of duty (moral obligation). This would not be so if the latter conception were definable in terms of the former. But Reid resists any attempt to reduce the moral principle to the principle of enlightened self-interest (rational self-love). The idea of duty is a simple, indefinable concept, a concept distinct from any notion of what is our good upon the whole (586–87). Although he believes that in a morally governed universe the two principles will not conflict, they remain distinct even in practice. For only when the agent is to some extent influenced to act from a sense of her duty does she merit moral approval.[2]

In what way then is the exercise of reason in making judgments required for Reid's second rational principle of action? Although Reid is not very explicit about this matter, I suspect the answer is this. The role of reason in the animal principles of action is to judge a course of conduct as the *means* to an end. But the judgment of whether a course of conduct is our duty is not as a means-end judgment, it is a judgment of the end itself to be pursued. To judge that a course of conduct (keeping promises, for example) is one's duty is to judge that that conduct is an *ultimate end,* something to be pursued for its own sake, and not a means to the realization of something else. Although the abstract notion of duty (obligation) may be conceived without reason being engaged in making judgments, it is by the exercise of reason in judging ultimate ends that anything is determined to be our duty.

Every deliberate human action must be done either as a means to some end or as an end for its own sake. Reid notes

2. Reid is careful to avoid the view that moral approval is merited only when a regard for duty is the *sole* motive for one's action.

that everyone agrees that it is the business of reason to determine the proper means to certain ends. What has been contended, particularly by Hume, is that reason cannot determine the ends to be pursued. Reid observes: "If this be so, reason cannot, with any propriety, be called a principle of action. Its office can only be to minister to the principles of action, by discovering the means of their gratification" (580). To establish a rational principle of action, therefore, Reid must show that the exercise of reason in making judgments is required either for forming the conception of the end to be pursued or for determining what things are to be pursued as ends in themselves. My suggestion is that the regard for our good upon the whole is a principle of action for which Reid thinks rational judgments are necessary in order to form the conception of the end; whereas the regard for our duty is a principle of action for which he thinks rational judgments are necessary in order to establish something (a course of conduct) as an end in itself.

Reid belongs to the moral sense school. He holds that our moral ideas are the product of a power (faculty). The exercise of this power results not only in our moral ideas of right and wrong, worth and fault, but also in our judgments that "this conduct is right, that is wrong; that this character has worth, that demerit" (590).[3] Judgments of right, wrong, and indifferent are directed at *actions;* judgments of worth or demerit are directed at *agents*. Some actions (action-types) are immediately perceived by our moral faculty to be right or wrong. The related moral judgments—Reid calls them "first principles of moral reasoning"—form the starting point for *moral reason-*

3. Reid stresses the analogy between the sense of morality (the moral sense) and the sense of perception. Just as the sense of perception is a source not only of certain ideas (the idea of the color red) but also of certain judgments (that object is red), so, too, the moral sense is a power that generates both moral ideas and moral judgments. For by the moral sense we perceive some things in human conduct to be right and others to be wrong. And to perceive that something is X is in part to judge that it is X.

ing, the process of reasoning from self-evident moral principles to conclusions that certain actions (particular or general) are morally right (obligatory), wrong, or indifferent. "Thus we shall find that all moral reasoning rests upon one or more first principles of morals, whose truth is immediately perceived without reasoning, by all men come to years of understanding" (591). As an example of a first principle in morals, Reid suggests: "That we ought not to do to another what we should think wrong to be done to us in like circumstances" (590). Reid claims that if a person cannot see the truth of this principle after reflecting on it seriously in a cool moment, that person is not a moral agent and cannot be convinced of the principle by rational argument.

Thus far we've seen that Reid holds a *deontological* theory of morals. He holds, that is, that the moral character of an action often depends on features of the action other than the good or bad consequences that will (or likely will) result from the performance of the action. But Reid does not think that the consequences of an action are never relevant to its moral character. For example, one of the first principles of morality he mentions is: "We ought to prefer a greater good, though more distant to a less; and a less evil to a greater" (638). It is not only foolish, against our interest, to choose the lesser immediate good over the greater but more distant good, it is also *morally wrong.* So, although clearly opposed to the view that conduciveness to our own greatest good is either the definition of duty or the single mark of its presence, Reid does think it is *a mark* of the presence of duty. But there are other marks of duty.

What is not quite so clear is whether Reid's theory is an *act*-deontological theory or a *rule*-deontological theory. According to the former, we directly intuit the rightness or wrongness (or indifference) of *particular actions* we consider doing. According to the latter, some general rules of conduct are directly apprehended by the mind and seen to be self-evident truths (the axioms of morality). The general tenor of his discussion fits more easily into the rule-deontological model, for the first principles he cites seem to be general rules governing actions. On the other hand, in speaking of the moral sense (moral faculty, conscience) Reid stresses the analogy to our other senses, particularly the power of determining by sight various properties of objects. Perhaps, then, just as by sight we discern that a particular object is red, so by conscience we perceive that a particular action is right.

I suspect that Reid is not an *act*-deontologist. Although he thinks that conscience often perceives a particular action to be right or wrong, it does so by seeing that the action is of a *kind* that it immediately recognizes as a kind of action that possesses the moral property of right (wrong). Other particular actions are not immediately recognized as being right (wrong). For these we must engage in moral reasoning from first principles and the circumstances that obtain. Because the circumstances of the agent and those affected by the action vary, the rightness (wrongness) of a particular action is always a contingent matter. But when the action and the circumstances are clear, we often can be certain of the judgment. When matters are more complicated, the best that can be had is a probable judgment of the moral character of a particular action under consideration. Reid gives as an example the case of the magistrate who knows that he ought to promote the good of the community but is uncertain as to which course of action will yield that result, and so he must depend on probable judgment.

Although moral propositions to the effect that this or that *particular* action is right, wrong, or indifferent are all contingent, some being certain for us and others only probable, the first principles of morality, according to Reid, are necessary truths.[4] As to what these fundamental duties are, Reid dis-

4. In his discussion of first principles, Reid divides them into contingent and necessary. The first principles of morality he cites as first principles of necessary truths (453–54).

tinguishes those that relate to duty in general (for example, we ought to use the best means we can to be well informed of our duty), those that relate to the different branches of duty, and those that determine precedence when duties conflict. Of those relating to the various branches of duty, Reid lists five, three of which are distinguished in terms of the object to which the duty is owed (oneself, other humans, God). The first is that each of us "ought to prefer a greater good, though more distant, to a less; and a less evil to a greater" (638). Curiously, this principle doesn't specify whose good we have an obligation to prefer, our own or that of others. But from Reid's discussion of the principle it is clear that he means our own good. In fact, his discussion makes it clear that it is the obtaining of the end of rational self-love (our own good upon the whole) that he is setting forth as a self-evident moral principle.[5] Presumably, then, when we satisfy ourselves that an action will serve our good as a whole we will be disposed to do that action out of a regard for our own best interest *and* out of a sense of duty. Moreover, if we have an obligation to secure our own interest, Reid's view of the coincidence of duty and self-interest is more plausible. For conscience cannot ever be in total opposition to rational self-love. And this is so regardless of whether our universe is morally governed. At most, the pursuit of our own good upon the whole might collide with *some other duty*.[6] Of course, we may still distinguish the person who pursues his greatest good from a sense of duty and the person who pursues his greatest good from a sense of his own interest, the former acting from a superior motive.

5. In discussing this first principle of morality, Reid notes that he had before observed that many ancient and modern moralists have sought to show that obedience to it leads to the practice of all the virtues (638). Looking back, we see that his reference is to the first rational principle of action, a regard to our good upon the whole (582–84).

6. It is surprising that in his earlier discussion of the two rational principles of action Reid gives not even a hint that one of our *duties* is the pursuit of our good upon the whole. For that it is one of our duties has a rather direct bearing upon his discussion of a possible conflict between the two principles.

We have a duty to seek the good of the society of humans and to do as much good and as little hurt as we can to the various human groups of which we are a part: family, friends, neighborhood, country, etc. In his discussion of the animal principles of action, Reid claims that we have a natural desire for the happiness of others, particularly those who are members of such groups, just as we have a natural desire for our own good. The latter, however, becomes a rational principle of action, because he sees that we have a desire for our own good upon the whole. But surely a similar desire may exist with respect to the well-being of others *on the whole*. But their good upon the whole, no less than our own, is an end of which we can form a conception only through the making of judgments. Had Reid moved in this direction, he would have ended with three rational principles of action: rational self-love, rational benevolence, and conscience. Moreover, the question would have had to be faced as to the rank-ordering of rational self-love and rational benevolence. By not raising the question of a desire for another's good upon the whole, Reid gains the superiority of self-love over benevolence simply on the grounds that the former is a rational principle of action, whereas the latter is an animal principle. But surely this is artificial. It is hardly credible that I should have a desire for the present happiness of my children and yet not desire their good upon the whole, once my reason has formed the conception of that good. But the latter would have to be a rational principle of conduct, given Reid's distinction between animal and rational principles. In any case, apart from their connection with duty, it is clear that Reid sees self-love as a superior principle to benevolence (when we consider benevolence as an animal principle), although, following Butler, he undoubtedly would stress the harmony between the two principles.[7]

Apart from the duty to venerate God, provided one be-

7. See Joseph Butler, *Fifteen Sermons*, sermons 11 and 12.

lieves in his existence and perfection, Reid completes his list of first principles with two other rules. One of them is: we ought to act toward another in the way we believe to be right for him to act toward us, if we were in his circumstances and he in ours. Sidgwick thinks this rule is nothing more than the formal rule that, quoting Reid, "right and wrong must be the same to all in all circumstances."[8] Undoubtedly Reid has in mind this formal principle of universalizability. But what he is after is something more than a merely formal principle. Reid's principle is that if A *judges* that it would be right (wrong) for B to do X to him (A) were their circumstances reversed, then it is right (wrong) for A to do X to B. The formal principle tells us that what is right (wrong) for me must be right (wrong) for another in the same circumstances. But it allows that it might be right for me to take your property even though I sincerely judge it would not be right for you to take mine were our circumstances reversed. All that follows from the formal principle is that my judgment about you would be mistaken. Reid's principle gives priority to our *judgment* of right (wrong) conduct in others for determining what is right (wrong) conduct in ourselves in the same circumstances. For we are "apt to be blinded by the partiality of selfish passions when the case concerns ourselves" (639). One of the defects of self-love is that it may cloud our vision of right and wrong when it is our own conduct that is under examination—thus the injunction to let our judgments of the conduct of those who are indifferent to us determine our judgment of our own conduct in the same circumstances. Although based on the formal principle noted above, Reid's principle is not identical with it.

Perhaps the most obscure of Reid's five axioms of morality

8. Henry Sidgwick, *Outlines of the History of Ethics* (London: Macmillan, 1954), 230. The quotation in Sidgwick is a mistake or a misprint. It should be as Reid puts it: "right and wrong must be the same to all in *the same* circumstances" (emphasis mine).

is the following: "As far as the intention of nature appears in the constitution of man, we ought to comply with that intention, and to act agreeably to it" (638). Our instincts and appetites are clearly intended by nature to assure our preservation. Other principles of action Reid believes also reveal nature's intention. He claims that the fact that we have benevolent affections toward others shows "that the author of our nature intended that we should live in society, and do good to our fellow-men as we have opportunity" (565). Seeing that nature has designed us for these ends, Reid concludes that we have a duty to act in a way that fosters these ends. Apart from the difficulty of determining that a principle of action is ours by nature rather than acquired and the difficulty of inferring the end for which such a principle of action was implanted in us, there is the larger problem of concluding that we *ought* to pursue ends because they *are* ends for which nature has designed us. Reid can appeal to God, the author of our nature, and our duty to obey him as the ground of our obligation to act agreeably to the intention of nature. But this would be to deduce the present principle from our duty to God. Reid's view, I take it, is that it is self-evident that it is wrong to act against our nature.

Although the principles of virtue are not themselves in conflict, they may lead to a conflict in action, one principle supporting a given action, another principle supporting a contrary action. Thus, our duty to benevolence may support an action of gratitude which the principle of justice forbids (Reid's example). So, if we are to reach unequivocal judgments as to the rightness or wrongness of a particular action, there must be axioms that dictate which principle should take precedence. Reid does little toward setting forth such principles, being content to note that justice takes precedence over gratitude, and gratitude preference over unmerited generosity (639).

When Reid tells us that the moral sense (conscience) is part of our constitution and that by which we both acquire moral ideas and perceive that certain actions are right and others wrong, he does not mean that from childhood we are all able to see the self-evidence of the first principles of morals; nor does he mean that each of us will be able to make these judgments when he comes "to years of understanding." He likens the progress of the body from infancy to maturity to the progress of the powers of the mind. Their development is the work of nature, but in both the work of nature "may be greatly aided or hurt by proper education. It is natural to man to be able to walk, or run, or leap; but, if his limbs had been kept in fetters from his birth, he would have none of those powers" (640). Hence, proper *instruction* and *practice* are necessary for the development of our powers, and the moral sense faculty is no exception. We do not expect someone to perceive immediately the self-evidence of the axiom that equals quantities added to equal quantities yield equal sums. The person must first acquire the relevant concepts of *more, less, equal,* etc. Then through experience and instruction she must become used to judging such matters in common life. When these developments have taken place the person may come to see the self-evidence of the mathematical axiom. In the same way, by practice and instruction she may come to see the self-evidence of the principles of morality.[9]

So far we've seen that the chief operations of conscience are to conceive of the notions of right, wrong, and indifferent and to perceive what things (action-types) have these unique properties. Let us suppose, then, that we perceive some proposed action to be our duty. Why should we perform that action which we judge to be our duty? Although Reid doesn't explicitly address this question it is clear, I think, that the question can be interpreted in at least three ways within his theory. We could take it to be the question: What moral obligation do we have to do what we are morally obligated to do?

9. See 595–96 for more from Reid on the need for education, practice, and habit in the development of the moral faculty.

So interpreted, the question doesn't merit discussion. Second, we can understand the question as: What motivation do we have to do what we perceive to be our duty? And, finally, we can imagine the question being raised in the context where it is clear that obtaining something we desire for its own sake conflicts with doing what we perceive to be our duty.

Reid claims that when we judge an action to be right or wrong, as opposed to judging it to be morally indifferent, we are so constituted that we feel some desire to do what is right and some desire to avoid doing what is wrong. Thus, we have a desire for a certain end, doing one's duty, that translates into a desire to do an action that we judge to be our duty. If we had no such desire toward duty for its own sake, conscience would not be a principle of action. It's true that Reid most often uses the phrase 'regard for duty' rather than 'desire for duty,' but he could as easily have spoken of a rational desire for pursuing our duty. So the answer to our second question is that the motivation to do what we perceive to be our duty rests on the fact that we are so constituted as to have a desire to do our duty. Doing our duty is something we desire for its own sake. It is, however, crucial to Reid's view that the desire for the object of either of the rational principles of action be sharply distinguished from the desire of the objects of our animal principles of action. For he insists that there is a profound difference between the ways in which the animal principles and the rational principles influence us to act. The animal principles act directly upon the will and give an impulse to act that can be resisted only by some effort on our part; whereas the rational principles are likened to advice, argument, and persuasion and are said to influence our judgment rather than our will (611). So, we need to look more deeply into our rational desire with respect to duty, if only to try to understand more clearly just what Reid takes it to be.

Reid tells us that we are so constituted as to *morally approve* of right conduct and to *morally disapprove* of wrong conduct. What this moral approval comes to is a complex of three items: a judgment that the conduct is right, a favorable affection toward the agent of the conduct, and some agreeable feeling in ourselves (592). It is the second item that I think is important to understanding his notion of "regard" for our duty. The affection that Reid thinks is felt toward the agent of right conduct he describes as "esteem" or "respect." Not only are we so constituted as to have this affection toward the agent of right conduct, but we immediately perceive that our esteem is properly due to such an agent.[10] In short, we *value* the person who acts from duty. And we value such an agent solely for the reason that the person acts from duty. Acting from duty, therefore, is an ultimate end, something that we value for its own sake.

My suggestion is that what makes the perception of our duty a principle of action for Reid is his view that we are so constituted that we value the moral agent, the person who acts from duty. The valuing of the moral agent *qua* moral agent consists in the esteem and goodwill we feel toward that agent. And when we perceive our own duty, we cannot but value ourselves as moral agents should we act from duty. It is this valuing of ourselves *qua* moral agents that inclines us to act from duty and thus constitutes the perception of our duty as a principle of action.

> But when a man, without thinking of himself more highly than he ought to think, is conscious of that integrity of heart and uprightness of conduct which he most highly esteems in others, and values himself duly upon this account, this, perhaps, may be called the pride of virtue; but it is not a vicious pride. It is a noble and magnanimous disposition without which there can be no steady virtue. (592)

10. We should note that it is not the mere doing of duty that merits this affection. For someone may do what ought to be done from some motive other than a regard for duty. In order for an agent to merit our moral esteem and respect, a regard for duty must have been one of his motives for doing what he did.

What of Reid's claim that the animal motives act directly upon the will and can be resisted only with effort, whereas the regard to duty acts on our judgment and is experienced as advice, exhortation, and argument rather than as an impulse to action? I take this to be a remark about the phenomenology of moral valuing as opposed to the phenomenology of our animal principles of action: the desire of food, power, etc. The felt difference is between the latter as 'drives' that impel us to action without thought or judgment and the former as 'judgments' that tell us that our moral worth is contingent upon acting from duty. A good part of this phenomenology is the ease with which we can avoid doing what duty demands, as opposed to the difficulty we have in resisting the demands of our animal desires. The same holds for our regard to our good upon the whole. The felt difference between a desire for some immediate pleasure and the valuing of our happiness upon the whole is like that between an immediate impulse to act and a judgment that such an action will be a matter of some regret later on. But in a good man, remorse for acting against duty is felt as painful and may be an influence toward doing one's duty.

Our study of Reid's moral theory would be incomplete without some account of his view that the moral rightness of an action depends on its being done from a sense of duty, from a sense that the action is right. Here are a few expressions of this doctrine and/or the broader view that it is the motive from which the action is done that determines the moral value of the action.

> The opinion of the agent in doing the action gives it its moral denomination. If he does a materially good action, without any belief of its being good, but from some other principle, it is no good action in him. And if he does it with the belief of its being ill, it is ill in him. (589)

> No action can be called morally good, in which a regard to what is right, has not some influence. Thus, a man who has no

> regard to justice, may pay his just debt, from no other motive but that he may not be thrown into prison. In this action there is no virtue at all. (98)

> That an action, done without any motive, can neither have merit nor demerit, is much insisted on by the writers for necessity, and triumphantly, as if it were the very hinge of the controversy. I grant it to be a self-evident proposition, and I know no author that ever denied it. (609–10)

> It appears evident, therefore, that those actions only can truly be called virtuous, or deserving of moral approbation, which the agent believed to be right, and to which he was influenced more or less, by that belief. (647)

It is the last of these expressions that merits some scrutiny. For what it appears to say is that what constitutes an action as *morally right* is the fact that the agent performs it from the conviction that it is morally right. And there seems to be something odd about this view. For how could doing A from the belief that A is morally right *make* A to be morally right? Either A is morally right or it is not. If it isn't, believing that it is won't make it so; and if it is, doing A from the belief that it is right cannot be necessary to A's being right. As Reid himself points out:

> When we judge an action to be good or bad, it must have been so in its own nature antecedent to that judgment, otherwise the judgment is erroneous. If, therefore, the action be good in its nature, the judgment of the agent cannot make it bad, nor can his judgment make it good if, in its nature, it be bad. For this would be to ascribe to our judgment a strange magical power to transform the nature of things, and to say, that my judging a thing to be what it is not, makes it really to be what I erroneously judge it to be. This, I think, is the objection in its full strength. (648)

Reid traces the objection to Hume. And before looking at Reid's reply, it will be instructive to note Hume's own statement of the objection. For Hume, no less than Reid, held that judgments of right and wrong are principally, if not solely, directed at the agent (or the agent's motives) and not at the external action the agent performed.

> 'Tis evident, that when we praise any actions, we regard only the motives that produced them, and consider the actions as signs or indications of certain principles in the mind and temper. The external performance has no merit. We must look within to find the moral quality. This we cannot do directly; and therefore fix our attention on actions, as on external signs. But these actions are still considered as signs; and the ultimate object of our praise and approbation is the motive, that produc'd them.[11]

Hume then argues that although the merit of the action is derived from the virtuous motive from which it is performed, it cannot be that this merit in the action is derived from a regard for the merit of the action.

> To suppose, that the mere regard to the virtue of the action, may be the first motive, which produc'd the action, and render'd it virtuous, is to reason in a circle. Before we can have such a regard, the action must be really virtuous; and this virtue must be deriv'd from some virtuous motive: And consequently the virtuous motive must be different from the regard to the virtue of the action. A virtuous motive is requisite to render an action virtuous. An action must be virtuous, before we can have a regard to its virtue. Some virtuous motive, therefore, must be antecedent to that regard.[12]

Hume is undoubtedly right in this argument. The difference between his argument and Reid's reconstruction of it is that

11. *Treatise of Human Nature,* book 3, part 2, sec. 1, 477.
12. *Treatise of Human Nature,* book 3, part 2, sec. 1, 478.

for 'a regard to the virtue of the action' Reid substitutes 'a conviction that the action is right.' The result is that the objection as recast by Reid is considerably weaker than it is in Hume. For Hume can use as a premise the following:

> An action must be virtuous, before we can have a regard to its virtue.

But Reid cannot use:

> An action must be virtuous, before we can have a conviction that it is virtuous.

Nevertheless, the objection is serious enough in the form that Reid gives to it to necessitate a reply.

Reid responds to Hume's objection by distinguishing *the moral worth of the action,* considered abstractly, apart from the agent's motive in performing it, from *the moral worth of the agent in performing that action.* The moral worth of the action itself is "inherent in its nature, and inseparable from it. No opinion or judgment of an agent can in the least alter its nature" (649). Thus, for example, the action of *relieving an innocent person who is suffering* has great moral worth, and its moral worth is intrinsic to it. But the moral worth of the agent who performs that action depends entirely on the motive in performing it. Suppose the agent relieves the innocent sufferer with the intention of plunging him into greater distress. Reid remarks: "In this action, there is surely no moral goodness, but much malice and inhumanity" (649). Given the distinction just drawn, what he really means here is that the agent, although he performs an action that is meritorious, has himself no merit at all in performing it but is actually a fit subject of moral blame, because he really *intended to do something* that is intrinsically very bad.[13] On the other hand, if the

13. It does not matter whether the agent succeeded in his intention. As long as he acted with the intention of doing what is intrinsically bad, believing it was in his power to do it, Reid believes he is morally guilty (*qua* agent) of the crime. "Nothing is more evident than that a man who tells the truth, believing it to be a lie, is guilty of falsehood; . . ." (648).

agent relieves the innocent sufferer from the sense of the rightness of the act, perhaps at some expense or danger to himself, then the agent is to be morally praised. But where lies the difference between these two cases? Not in the external action, Reid claims, because that is common to the two cases. The difference lies in the motive from which the action was done.

Reid's solution makes good sense. Any remaining problem stems from his talk of *the action* of our first agent as morally bad, assuming that all that the agent actually managed to do was relieve the innocent sufferer. (We will suppose he was unable to plunge the innocent person into greater distress.) For it hardly seems correct in any literal sense to describe the action of relieving an innocent sufferer as morally bad. Reid, I think, would agree with this point: "But when a man exerts his active power well or ill, there is a moral goodness or turpitude which we *figuratively impute to the action,* but which is truly and properly imputable to the man only; and this goodness or turpitude depends very much upon the intention of the agent, and the opinion he had of his action" (649, emphasis mine).

Reid claims that the basic distinction he has made to solve this puzzle has long been understood by those who have written about moral theory. "In the scholastic ages, an action good in itself was said to be *materially* good, and an action done with a right intention was called *formally* good. This last way of expressing the distinction is still familiar among Theologians; but Mr. Hume seems not to have attended to it, or to have thought it to be words without any meaning" (649–50). What is not quite so clear is where Reid stands with respect to the agent who does a materially bad act with a very good intention. If one performs a materially good act from a bad intention, one's action (figuratively), as well as oneself (*qua* agent of that act), is morally bad. But if one does a materially bad act with the intention of doing good, is the agent's action (figuratively), as well as oneself (*qua* agent of that act), morally good? Perhaps here Reid would follow Aquinas and give a negative answer.[14] In any case, it should be clear both that Reid's distinction provides a solution to Hume's objection and is consistent with Reid's persistent view that, quite apart from the motive from which it is done, an action has an intrinsic moral character of right, wrong, or indifferent. But in the light of Reid's solution to Hume's objection, I think we can see that Reid's doctrine is expressed in a rather misleading way. For his statement of the doctrine is as follows:

> Those actions only can truly be called virtuous, or deserving of moral approbation, which the agent believed to be right, and to which he was influenced more or less, by that belief. (647)

But given the distinction, what he means by this doctrine is more clearly expressed as

> Whether the action is materially good or bad, the agent who performs it deserves moral approbation for performing it only if the agent believed the action to be right and was influenced in performing it by that belief.

14. *Summa Theologica,* Ia, IIae, 20, 2.

8

Objections to Libertarian Freedom: 1

The fantasy of a power to declare one's independence, not only of inclination, but of reason itself within and of good and evil without, is sometimes painted in such fine colours that one might take it to be the most excellent thing in the world. Nevertheless it is only a hollow fantasy. . . . What is asserted is impossible, but if it came to pass it would be harmful.

—Leibniz

"What is asserted is impossible, but if it came to pass it would be harmful."[1] This remark by Leibniz nicely captures most of the objections to the view of Reid and other free will advocates. For these objections divide into those that claim that libertarian freedom is impossible because it is internally inconsistent, or inconsistent with some well-established principle of causality or explanation, and those that claim that the possession of free will would be harmful because the agent's actions would be uninfluenced by motives and therefore capricious, ungovernable, and unaffected by rewards or punishment. In this chapter we will examine some objections of the first type, reserving objections of the second type for the last chapter. Although I believe Reid has decisively answered sev-

1. Leibniz aimed this remark at Archbishop King's version of libertarianism (*Theodicy*, 406).

eral objections of both types, I will argue that his version of libertarianism is not without significant difficulties.

We can begin with two objections whose purpose is to show that Reid's libertarian theory implies the absurdity that each act of will that is free is itself the result either of a prior act of will, ad infinitum (first objection), or of a prior exertion of power, ad infinitum (second objection). The first of these, by far the more popular, is, I believe, a spurious objection. According to the free will position, an action is free provided it is willed and the agent freely determined or brought about that act of will. But, so the spurious objection goes, to freely determine an act of will is to freely will that act of will. So an act of will is freely determined only if it is freely chosen. But an agent freely chooses an act of will only if his choice of that act of will is itself freely determined by the agent, in which case the choice of the act of will is itself the result of a prior free choice by the agent. And so we are off to the races, each free determination of the will by the agent being preceded by an infinite series of determinations of the will by the agent. This objection, which Reid traces to Hobbes (601), fails, however, because it supposes that what it is for the agent to freely determine his will (that is, bring it about that he wills X rather than something else) is for the agent to freely *will* that his will be determined in a certain manner.[2] But it is very doubtful that any free will advocate held this view. Many libertarians attributed to the agent a power of self-determination, a self-moving principle. But by this they meant only that, when the volitional act is produced by the self-moving principle, it is produced by the agent himself and not by any other thing or agent.[3] They did not mean that in causing his volition the agent first chose or willed to produce that volition. To at-

2. This assumption of what it is for an agent to freely determine his will can be found in Jonathan Edwards, *Freedom of the Will,* 172.

3. See "Unpublished Letters of Thomas Reid to Lord Kames, 1762–1782," collected by Ian Simpson Ross, *Texas Studies in Literature and Language* 7 (1965): 51.

tribute such a view to them is to misunderstand what they claimed. According to the free will advocates, the soul or mind determines the will but does not do so by choosing or willing that the mind will X rather than some other act. To freely bring about a volition is nothing more than for the agent to exert her power to cause that volition. The exertion of power is not itself a volition.

The second objection, however, is serious, revealing, I believe, a real difficulty in Reid's agent-cause account of freedom. Like the first, this objection also arrives at the absurd conclusion that any action requires an infinite series of antecedent events, each produced by the agent who produces the action. This absurd conclusion, I believe, does follow from Reid's view of agent-causation in conjunction with the principle that every event has a cause. I propose here to explain how this absurdity is embedded in Reid's theory and what can be done to remove or subdue it.

On Reid's theory, when an agent wills some action, the act of will is itself an event and, as such, requires a cause.[4] If the act of will is free, its cause is not some event, it is the agent whose act of will it is. Being the cause of the act of will, the agent must satisfy Reid's three conditions of agent-causation. Thus the agent must have had the power to bring about the act of will and the power to refrain from bringing about the act of will and must have *exerted* her power to bring about the act of will. It is the last of these conditions that generates an infinite regress of events that an agent must cause if she is to cause her act of will. For what it tells us is that to produce the act of will the agent must *exert* her power to bring about the act of will. Now an exertion of power is itself an event. As such, it too must have a cause. On Reid's view the cause must again be the agent herself. But to have caused this exertion, the agent must have had the power to bring it about and must have *exerted* that power. Each exertion of power is itself an event which the

4. "I consider the determination of the will as an effect" (602).

agent can cause only by having the power to cause it and by *exerting* that power. As Reid reminds us, "In order to the production of any effect, there must be in the cause, not only power, but the exertion of that power: for power that is not exerted produces no effect" (603). The result of this principle, however, is that, in order to produce any act of will whatever, the agent must cause an infinite number of exertions. When conjoined with the principle that every event has a cause, Reid's theory of agent-causation leads to the absurdity of an infinite regress of agent-produced exertions for every act of will the agent produces.

It is (from one point of view) remarkable that Reid appears never to have seen this difficulty in his theory. Occasionally he joins the causal principle and his view of agent-causation into a single remark, with the result that the difficulty fairly leaps up from the page. For example, in discussing Leibniz's view that every action has a sufficient reason, Reid remarks: "If the meaning of the question be, was there a cause of the action? Undoubtedly there was: of every event there must be a cause, that had power sufficient to produce it, and that exerted that power for the purpose" (625). If exertions of power are events—and what else could they be?—the infinite regress of exertions produced by the agent who performs any action is abundantly apparent in this remark. Perhaps Reid didn't see the problem because he always had in mind the basic distinction between the *effects* agents produce by their actions and the *actions* of the agents by which they produce those effects. With this distinction in mind, it is natural to suppose that *everything* an agent causes (the effects) she causes not simply by virtue of having a certain power but by acting, by exerting that power. Put this way, Reid's notion that an agent can cause something only by acting, by *exerting* her power, is intuitively attractive. So attractive, perhaps, that one may be blind to the difficulty that appears when actions, by virtue of being events, are themselves held to be among the things an agent causes.

I can think of only three possible responses to this objection. First, we can simply accept the absurdity of an infinite regress of exertions of power whenever the agent causes an act of will.[5] Second, we can hold that the agent's exertion of power in producing an act of will is an event that has no efficient cause at all, thus abandoning the causal principle. Finally, we can take the view that the agent's exertion of power in producing an act of will is not an *event* and therefore does not fall under the causal principle that every event has an efficient cause. Not falling under that principle, there is no need to insist that the agent must cause her exertion of power by a preceding exertion of power, ad infinitum.

Of the three responses, I want to begin by exploring the third, for it requires the fewest changes in Reid's theory. But since Reid seems oblivious to the problem raised by this objection, the reader should be aware that it is speculation on my part that the third response is the most appropriate to pursue, even from the point of view of sustaining both Reid's theory of agent-causation and his principle that every event has an efficient (agent-) cause.

As we've seen, the serious objection focuses on two elements in Reid's theory. The first is that when an agent causes an act of will (or anything else) she does so by virtue of having the power to cause it and *exerting that power.* The second element is that every event is caused by some agent. Putting these two together forces us to find the agent as the cause of *the exertion of power* that produces her act of will. For an exertion of power is surely just as much an *event* as the act of will the agent produces by that exertion of power. But is it? Does Reid really mean to hold that the agent's exertion of power is itself an event and therefore something the agent must cause

5. When Chisholm was defending agent-causation, he embraced for a time this sort of response, playing down the charge that such a regress was an absurdity. See, for example, "Some Puzzles about Agency," in *The Logical Way of Doing Things,* ed. Karel Lambert (New Haven: Yale University Press, 1969), 206, and "On the Logic of Intentional Action," in *Agent, Action and Reason,* ed. Robert Binkeley et al. (Toronto: University of Toronto Press, 1971), 47.

by another exertion of power? Since to my knowledge Reid never addresses this question, we can only speculate. Here, then, is my speculation. Suppose Reid had never claimed that every *event* has an efficient cause. Or suppose we simply ignore that *particular claim* and consider only the more fully stated causal principles he announces. What we are left with is this:

> Everything that begins to exist, must have a cause of its existence, which had power to give it existence. And every thing that undergoes any change, must have some cause of that change. (603)[6]

Let's focus on the second causal principle. Reid tells us that from this principle it follows that if a being *undergoes a change* then either that being itself is the efficient cause of the change it undergoes, in which case it has *active power* and *acts* in producing that change, or some other being is the efficient cause of the change, in which case the being undergoing the change is merely passive, acted upon, the active power being only in that being that produced the change. What is it for a being to *act* in producing some change that it undergoes? It is nothing more than for that being to have power to produce that change and to exert that power. "All that is necessary to the production of any effect, is power in an efficient cause to produce the effect, and the exertion of that power; . . ." (603). Now my speculation is that, apart from a thing's coming into existence, Reid believes that it is only the *changes things undergo* that require causes. A volition occurring in a person is a change that person undergoes. And if the person herself is the efficient cause of that change, then she *acted* in producing

6. Immediately following this remark, Reid adds: "*That neither existence, nor any mode of existence, can begin without an efficient cause,* is a principle that appears very early in the mind of man; and it is so universal, and so firmly rooted in human nature, that the most determined scepticism cannot eradicate it" (603).

it. Her acting to produce that volition is simply her exerting her power to produce that change (the occurrence of the volition) within herself. Now the exertion of power, unlike the volition, is not a change she undergoes; for it is her own activity, her own exercise of active power. As such, it does not require a cause. The exertion of our active power by which we produce some change in us is not itself a change in us that we undergo. Therefore, it is not the sort of thing for which Reid's causal principles would require a cause.

To support this line of reasoning, I offer what I regard as a compelling argument for the view that the exertion of power by which an agent produces an effect cannot itself be an effect produced by an efficient cause. For suppose it were. Suppose, following Reid's remark about volitions, I say: "I consider the exertion of active power as an effect." If so, then like my volition that could be produced in me by God or some other efficient cause, my exertion of active power in bringing about something could be caused by God or some other efficient cause distinct from me. But it is a *conceptual impossibility* within Reid's theory for God or any other efficient cause to produce in me an exertion of my active power. For my exertion of active power in producing something is identical with my agent-causing that thing. And, as we saw in Chapter 4, it is impossible that I should be caused to agent-cause anything. If x causes y to cause something, then y does not have the power *not* to cause that thing. And an agent has power to cause only if he has power not to cause. For Reid this is a conceptual truth. "Power to produce any effect, implies power not to produce it" (523).

We've just looked at two arguments. According to the first, the only changes in an agent for which Reid's causal principles require an efficient cause are changes the agent undergoes. But an exertion of active power is an activity of an agent, not a change the agent undergoes. According to the second argument, if God or some other being were to cause my exertion of power, it would necessitate my agent-causing whatever is produced by that exertion of power. But this would mean that it was not in my power not to produce that thing. And this conflicts with one of the essential features of agent causation: "Power to produce an effect supposes power not to produce it; otherwise it is not power but necessity, which is incompatible with power in the strict sense" (65). The first argument justifies us in holding that Reid's causal principles do not require that there be an efficient cause of an exertion of active power. The second argument justifies us in holding the stronger view that, given Reid's conditions for agent-causation, there could not be an efficient cause of an exertion of active power.

It must be admitted that what I've said to be justified by the second argument goes somewhat beyond its conclusion. For all the argument strictly precludes is that some *other being* should be the efficient cause of my exertion of active power. Could not I be the efficient cause of my own exertion of active power? If I am its efficient cause, then it was in my power to produce that effect (the exertion of power), and I exerted my power for that purpose.[7] But once I have exerted my power to bring about the original exertion of power, the original exertion of power is causally necessitated, and it is not in my power not to cause whatever is to be produced by the original exertion of power. So once again we encounter the same impossibility. If there is an efficient cause of my exertion of active power, then, given the operation of that efficient cause (whether it be me or some other being), my exertion of active power is causally necessitated, and it is not in my power not to cause whatever is the causal product of that exercise of active power. In short, that exercise of active power is not an exercise of active power. I take it as established, therefore, that (1) Reid's principles about what requires an efficient cause do not include the agent's

7. "In the strict and proper sense, I take an efficient cause to be a being who had power to produce the effect, and exerted that power for that purpose" (letter to Dr. James Gregory [65]).

exercise of active power and that (2) given the conditions Reid lays down for agent-causation, it is conceptually impossible that there should be an efficient cause of an agent's exercise of active power.

The conclusions just reached, however, ignore that (a) an exertion of active power certainly appears to be an event and that (b) Reid declares that every event has an efficient cause. How then can we credit the arguments just given to show that Reid's true view is that an exertion of active power is the activity of an agent and as such has no efficient cause? My suggestion (speculation) is that Reid is using 'event' to denote just what his more elaborate principles specify: the coming into existence of a substance; any change that a substance undergoes. This suggestion is, perhaps, *ad hoc.*[8] But the result is that a solution is possible for the serious infinite regress objection, a solution that leaves the fundamental themes of Reid's agency theory intact. No major surgery on his system is required.

Another possible support for the view that the agent's exercise of his active power is not itself a change in the agent may be contained in Aristotle's remarks about a *self-mover.* A self-mover is distinguished from a moved-mover. The latter (for example, a stick moving a stone) has a capacity to bring about movement in something else (the stone), but the exercise of that capacity is itself a movement. The *exercise* of the moved-mover's capacity to bring about motion in another is therefore an event. But the agent who causes the stick to move must be an unmoved-mover—the exercise of its capacity to cause movement in another is *not itself a movement.* Not being a movement, it is not a change in a substance and is therefore

8. In one of his letters to Dr. Gregory there is some slight indication that Reid may have taken an event to be nothing more than a change a thing undergoes. But at best this is only one reading of the following remark: "I apprehend that there is one original notion of *cause* grounded in human nature, and that this is the notion on which the maxim is grounded—that every change or event must have a cause" (75).

not an event. Thus Aristotle appears to hold that a *self-mover* has a part that is moved (undergoes a change) and a part that moves but is not itself in motion (does not undergo a change). The part that moves but is not itself in motion must, of course, *exercise* its capacity to produce motion in the part that is moved. But this *exercise* of the unmoved part's capacity to produce motion is not itself a change in the part that is not itself in motion (not itself a change in the part that is an unmoved-mover).[9] Following Aristotle we might take Reid to hold that the exercise of the agent's power to produce the volition to do A is *not itself* a change in the agent; it is not a change the agent undergoes. Now the causal principle, as Reid interprets it, holds that every event (every change in a substance) has a cause. The exertion of power to produce a *basic change* (for example, an act of will), however, is not itself a change the substance undergoes. Therefore, it is not an event and therefore does not require a cause. It would be an interesting and important addition to historical scholarship to see if Reid's theory can bear this interpretation.

For those modern philosophers who, like me, would hold that an exertion of power, no less than an act of will, is a change in an agent and therefore an event, the only conclusion the above arguments will permit is that Reid is, after all, an indeterminist. Not all events have efficient causes. In particular, any event that consists in an exertion of active power will lack an efficient cause. The important point that has emerged, however, is that *Reid's theory precludes an efficient cause of an exertion of active power by an agent.* And this point provides the solution to the infinite regress of causes (the serious objection). Of less importance is the matter of whether or not an exertion of active power qualifies as an event. If it does, Reid

9. See Aristotle's *Physics,* book 8, sec. 4 and 5. For a quite different interpretation of Aristotle's view of the self-mover, see John Thorp, *Free Will: A Defense against Neurophysiological Determinism* (London: Routledge & Kegan Paul, 1980), 96–99.

is an indeterminist. If it does not, Reid is not an indeterminist, for every event has an efficient cause.

It is instructive to note some consequences of viewing an exertion of active power as an event. First, as we've seen, we must then take Reid to be an indeterminist, for the event that is the agent's exertion of active power cannot be caused. Second, Reid must be viewed as a special sort of indeterminist, for we must understand him as holding that every event that logically can have a cause does have a cause. Third, we should not confuse Reidian indeterminism with what I will call "simple indeterminism." According to simple indeterminism, the uncaused event is the act of will resulting in the action or some other intentional act such as an agent's undertaking something.[10] But an act of will or an undertaking is the sort of event that can be caused by other agents or events. Reid's exertion of active power is not the sort of event that can be caused. I believe the agent-causation theory advanced by Reid has an advantage over simple indeterminism. For Reid's theory has a built-in answer to the question: Why is the event of the agent's exertion of power uncaused? Simple indeterminism has no answer to the corresponding question of why the act of will is uncaused.

Fourth, as a corollary to the last point, we should note that an exertion of active power is intrinsically more truly an agent's *own action* than is an act of will. Both events, of course, are doings of the agent. When something else produces in me an act of will to turn on my computer, it is true that *I* will to turn on my computer. But this act of will is *less my own activity* than it would be were I the cause of it.[11] What makes me the cause of my act of will is my exercising my active power to

10. For an account of an agent's undertaking something, see Roderick Chisholm, *Person and Object* (La Salle, Ill.: Open Court, 1976), 53–84.

11. For those who take the cause of a particular act of will to be essential to it, the point would be the following. An act of will in me that is caused by something else is less truly my own act than is an act of will in me that is caused by me.

bring it about. Since the latter is what makes an act of will more truly my own act and since no other agent can cause in me that exercise of active power, nothing can be more truly *my own act* than my exercise of active power. And this remains so even though I do not cause my exercise of active power.[12]

Finally, we should note that by taking the agent's exertion of active power as an event we can dispel some of the mystery about agent-causation that many philosophers feel nowadays. According to some recent advocates of agent-causation, there is an irreducible causal relation binding a substance (the agent) to an event (the act of will).[13] One apparent trouble with the notion of such an irreducible causal relation is that the act of will takes place at a particular time; whereas the agent that causes it is an enduring substance. As Baruch Brody puts it: "After all, the agent presumably existed for a long time before that particular act of willing, so it is not the mere existence of the agent that produces the act of willing. What then causes the act of willing to take place when it does? The answer to this question is the missing link in Reid's theory of human liberty."[14] I believe this is a confusion in an otherwise excellent introduction to Reid's *Essays*. When Reid says that the agent is the cause of the act of will, he does not mean that we are left with nothing more than an enduring substance that mysteriously brings about an event (an act of will) *without doing anything to bring it about.* A person agent-causes

12. In the next chapter, I argue that even though nothing causes an exercise of active power, its occurrence is *up to* the agent whose exercise it is.

13. See, for example, Roderick Chisholm, "Freedom and Action," in *Freedom and Determinism,* ed. Keith Lehrer (New York: Random House, 1966), 16–23. Also see Richard Taylor, *Action and Purpose* (Englewood Cliffs, N.J.: Prentice-Hall, 1966), 99–138.

14. Baruch Brody, introduction, *Essays on the Active Powers of the Human Mind,* by Thomas Reid (Cambridge, Mass.: MIT Press, 1969), xix. The same criticism and others are advanced by Irving Thalberg, *Misconceptions of Mind and Freedom* (New York: University Press of America, 1983), 153–184. Also see Carl Ginet's endorsement of this criticism in Ginet, *On Action* (Cambridge: Cambridge University Press, 1990), 13–14.

her act of will by exercising her active power to bring about that act of will. The exercise of her active power is an event. It is incorrect, therefore, to suppose that when a person agent-causes her act of will the only event to be found in the neighborhood of the agent is the act of will. Without the exercise of active power there can be no occurrence of the act of will (assuming that the agent is truly the cause of the volition). Indeed, Reid says as much: "so every change must be caused by some exertion, or by the cessation of some exertion of power. That which produces a change by the exertion of its power, we call the *cause* of that change; and the change produced, the *effect* of that cause" (515).

Although Brody is incorrect in his representation of Reid's theory, it would be a mistake, I believe, to take the correction I have made as implying that no events are *directly caused* by the agent. The fact that the agent causes her act of will by exercising her active power to bring about that act of will should not be understood to imply that the agent causes her act of will by causing some other event that event-causes the act of will. Often enough, the agent does cause an event by causing some other event that event-causes the event in question. I cause my action of breaking the window by causing my action of throwing the brick against the window. The latter action causes the former.[15] But if agent-causation is correct, there must be some event the agent *directly causes* in the sense that there is nothing else the agent causes that brings about that event.[16] On Reid's theory, the event the agent directly causes is the act of will.

15. Actually, this is something of an oversimplification. The event that event-causes another event will be rather complex, since it must be physically necessary that given it the second event occurs. Also, following Goldman, we should perhaps say that the second action "causally generates" the first (Alvin Goldman, *A Theory of Human Action* [Englewood Cliffs, N.J.: Prentice-Hall, 1970], 20–25).

16. Compare Chisholm's view of an agent's undertaking as something the agent brings about directly (*Person and Object*, 84–85).

To avoid an infinite regress, we must suppose that whenever a person agent-causes anything, there is some event e he agent-causes without causing any other event that event-causes e. In Reid's theory, e is an act of will. In response to Brody, we've observed that directly causing an act of will does not mean that we are left with *only* the agent, the act of will, and some mysterious claim that the former caused the latter. The agent directly causes the act of will by exerting his active power to bring it about. So we have two events: the act of will that is caused by the agent; and the exertion of active power by the agent in producing that act of will. Does the fact that the latter event is distinct from the act of will imply that the agent does not directly cause that act of will? No. For even if we took the exercise of active power to cause the act of will, we must remember that neither the agent nor anything else can cause the exercise of active power. So it won't be true that the agent causes the act of will by *causing* some other event that event-causes that act of will.

The one remaining question we face here is this: When the agent exercises her active power to bring about her act of will, does the event which is her exercise of active power to bring about her act of will *event-cause* her act of will? If the answer to this question is affirmative, then we can plausibly claim that agent-causation is reducible to event-causation. For whenever a person directly causes some act of will, it will be true that an event involving that agent (an exercise of active power) event-causes that act of will. In theory, then, we could replace agent-causation talk ("The person agent-caused her act of will") with event-causation talk ("An exercise of active power in the person event-caused her act of will").

My answer to the above question is no. I take it that event-causation of e′ by e requires that e and e′ are events such that if e occurs at t it is physically necessary but not logically necessary that e′ occurs at t or after t.[17] An exercise of active power

17. See Chisholm, *Person and Object*, 58–59.

to bring about e is an event such that if it occurs it is *logically necessary* that e occurs. As Reid remarks: "All that is necessary to the production of any effect, is power in an efficient cause to produce the effect, and the exertion of that power; for it is a *contradiction* to say, that the cause has power to produce the effect, and exerts that power, and yet the effect is not produced" (603, emphasis mine). On Reid's theory, then, it is logically impossible that the following statements should both be true:

> S exerted his active power to bring about e at t.
> e did not occur at t.[18]

We've now considered two views of the exercise of active power. According to the one view that I have suggested may have been Reid's, the exercise of active power is not an event. According to the second account (the one I hold), it is an event. Suffice it to remark here that on either account there is a legitimate question of explanation that is left dangling in Reid's account of an agent-cause. If we take the route of treating the exertion of active power as a genuine event without an efficient cause, thus making Reid an indeterminist, there is the question of why that event occurred. How are we to explain it, given that it lacks an efficient cause? If we take the route I've suggested Reid may have held, viewing the exertion of power as the activity of the agent, something distinct from an event (change undergone), there is the question of why the agent engaged in that exertion of power at that moment of

18. Perhaps in directly causing her volition there is an exercise of power that event-causes the volition. If so, then we can reduce agent-causation talk to event-causation talk. I see no great harm in this to the theory of agent-causation. What will remain the distinguishing feature of agent-causation is the relation of the unique event, *the agent's exercise of active power,* to the agent. As we shall see in the next chapter, any such event has the property that its occurrence is *up to the agent.* And this last is true even though the exercise of active power is uncaused.

time. How are we to explain the agent's then exerting his power, given that it is an occasion of agent-causing and cannot itself have an efficient cause? We will return to this problem in the next chapter.

The two infinite regress arguments we've been considering are meant to show that libertarian freedom is impossible. Another argument intended to establish inconsistency rests on the claim that libertarian freedom conflicts with some metaphysical principle of explanation or some principle of universal causation. As an instance of the former, Reid mentions Leibniz's Principle of Sufficient Reason: "For every existence, for every event, for every truth, there must be a sufficient reason."[19] As an instance of the latter, Reid notes the claim that every event has a cause. Reid responds to the first by noting that in one sense the libertarian will admit, if not insist, that a free act of will has a sufficient reason. For if a sufficient reason of a free act of will is nothing more than a cause of it, then the libertarian will embrace the principle's application to free acts of will. But by 'cause,' of course, the libertarian will mean an efficient or agent-cause. If, on the other hand, a sufficient reason of a free action (or free act of will) is taken to be "something previous to the action, which made it to be necessarily produced," Reid's response is that the Principle of Sufficient Reason simply begs the question against the libertarian. He makes a similar response to the proponent of universal causation. So long as the agent is allowed to be the cause of the free action, the libertarian has no quarrel with the principle of universal causation. But if by 'cause' is meant something in the previous circumstances that is constantly followed by a certain effect, Reid acknowledges that the libertarian must regard a free volition as an event without a cause.[20] So if we interpret a 'sufficient reason' or a 'cause' as

19. Cited by Reid, 624.

20. Reid quotes Joseph Priestley as advocating this definition of 'cause,' a definition that Reid thinks is quite close to Hume's account (627).

an agent-cause, the libertarian has no objection to the Principle of Sufficient Reason or the Principle of Universal Causation. But if by 'sufficient reason' or 'cause' is meant some previous event or circumstance that necessitates its effect, then the libertarian responds that, unless proven, the principles simply beg the question against the libertarian position. Reid readily admits that "When it is proved that, through all nature, the same consequences invariably result from the same circumstances, the doctrine of liberty must be given up" (626).[21] But short of a proof of such a thesis, the libertarian is certainly within her rights to reject the principles when 'cause' is being used in the sense espoused by Hume, Priestley, and others. With some justification, then, Reid concludes his discussion of the arguments against the possibility of libertarian freedom by remarking:

> Every argument in a dispute, which is not grounded on principles granted by both parties, is that kind of sophism which logicians call *petitio principii;* and such, in my apprehension, are all the arguments offered to prove that liberty of action is impossible (628).[22]

21. For an illuminating discussion of why this is so in Reid's theory, see Keith Lehrer, *Thomas Reid* (London: Routledge and Kegan Paul, 1989), 283–87.

22. I cite this remark with approval, but it must be admitted that Reid often presents arguments against the skeptics that are grounded on principles that the skeptics themselves would not accept. His remark, therefore, should be understood within the limits of the philosophy of common sense. It is not intellectually wrong to use an argument grounded in some basic belief of common sense against an opponent who does not accept those common-sense beliefs. Undoubtedly, however, Reid would say that whatever the official position of the opponent of common-sense beliefs may be, that opponent, like everyone else, cannot but believe the deliverances of common sense (see 618–20).

9

Objections to Libertarian Freedom: 2

One will have it that the will is alone active and supreme, and one is wont to imagine it to be like a queen seated on her throne, whose minister of state is the understanding, while the passions are her courtiers or favourite ladies, who by their influence often prevail over the counsel of her ministers. One will have it that . . . she can vacillate between the arguments of the minister and the suggestions of the favourites, even rejecting both, making them keep silence or speak, and giving them audience or not as seems good to her. But it is a personification or mythology somewhat ill-conceived.

—Leibniz

In the last chapter we noted an apparent difficulty in Reid's agency theory, a difficulty concerning the agent's exercise of his active power to produce some action or change. How are we to *explain* that exercise of power, given that it lacks a cause?[1] And, as we noted, this problem confronts us whether or not we adopt my view that an exercise of active power is an event. For, even if we suppose it not to be an event, it is an instance of agent-causing, and no instance of agent-causing can itself be caused. Since the problem of explaining its occurrence remains, whether or not the exercise of active power is an event, I will proceed by taking it to be an

1. This problem, of course, is not unique to Reid's theory. Every theory holding that indeterminism is essential to the exercise of genuine freedom encounters it in one form or another.

event, thus taking Reid (against his will, perhaps) to be an indeterminist.

Proponents of agent-causation have sometimes argued that freedom and responsibility require us to reject indeterminism. Thus, in one of his early discussions of agent-causation, after giving the usual libertarian argument to show that determinism conflicts with moral responsibility, Roderick Chisholm remarks:

> Perhaps there is less need to argue that the ascription of responsibility also conflicts with an indeterministic view of action—with the view that the act, or some event that is essential to the act, is not caused at all. If the act—the firing of the shot—was not caused at all, if it was fortuitous or capricious, happening so to speak "out of the blue," then, presumably, no one—and nothing—was responsible for the act. Our conception of action, therefore, should be neither deterministic nor indeterministic. Is there any other possibility?[2]

Chisholm proposed to avoid both determinism and indeterminism by holding that some event essential to the act is not caused by any other event but is caused by the agent. To the question that has perplexed Brody and others—what does the agent *do* to bring about that event? (see the last chapter)—Chisholm responded (unlike Reid, I believe) by saying that the agent does nothing. But what then is the difference between the event simply happening in the agent and the agent causing that event? Chisholm could only say the difference is that in the second case the event is caused.[3]

What if we focus on the event of the person agent-causing that event? What caused *that* event? If it was determined by earlier events, then the agent can't be responsible for it and

2. "Freedom and Action," in *Freedom and Determinism,* ed. Keith Lehrer (New York: Random House, 1966), 16.

3. "Freedom and Action," 21.

can't therefore be responsible for the event he originally agent-caused and for what it causes. Did it simply happen out of the blue? Chisholm's answer was to adopt the general principle that for any event e, if S agent-causes e, then S agent-causes the event that is S agent-causing e.[4] Thus we are off to the races with an infinite number of agent-causings whenever the agent agent-causes anything.

Our brief look at Chisholm's early version of agency theory has disclosed two difficulties that I believe are unavoidable for agent-causation so long as it insists on denying indeterminism.[5] Neither of these difficulties afflicts the view of Reid's theory that is being advocated here.[6] For we've seen that when the person is the direct cause of some event, the agent causes that event by doing something: exercising her active power to bring about that event. And we've also seen that neither the agent nor anything else can be the cause of the agent's exercise of active power, thus forestalling an infinite regress of agent-causings.

We now face the second set of objections we noted at the beginning of the last chapter: those that argue that the possession of libertarian freedom would be harmful because the agent's actions would be uninfluenced by motives and therefore capricious, ungovernable, and unaffected by reward or punishment. The core idea in this set of objections is that if an agent has libertarian freedom and nothing causes her to agent-cause her action, then her action must be *uninfluenced*

4. See Radu J. Bogdan, ed., *Roderick M. Chisholm* (Dordrecht: D. Reidel, 1986), 63–64.

5. Actually, what I say here assumes that an exercise of active power is an *event.* This assumption is not always pointed out in the following discussion.

6. These criticisms of Chisholm's early version of agent-causation fail to take account (1) of his imaginative and interesting defense of this early view and (2) of the significant changes Chisholm later made to his theory. Should my brief discussion here appear somewhat dismissive, let me say that I have learned more from the study of Chisholm's writings on this subject than from the writings of any other philosopher, with the possible exception of Thomas Reid.

by motives. Clearly, this objection is closely tied to the problem I mentioned at the outset of this chapter: How are we to *explain* the exercise of active power, given that it lacks a cause? Before turning to the question about the influence of motives, however, it will be helpful to consider the more basic problem of how the agent can be *responsible* for her exercise of active power, given that it has no cause.[7] As we noted, the early Chisholm worried that an uncaused event would be capricious, arbitrary, something that happens "out of the blue." If these things are so, how can we possibly hold the agent responsible for any exercise of her active power, or any action she brings about by exercising her active power?

The reasoning against the agent being responsible for an exercise of active power is as follows:

1. The agent's exercise of active power is uncaused.
therefore,
2. The agent's exercise of active power is fortuitous or capricious.
therefore,
3. The agent is not responsible for his exercise of active power.

Is this reasoning sound? Clearly, if something's taking place is fortuitous or capricious, I can't very well be responsible for it. But what of the inference from (1) to (2)? Given that the agent's exercise of active power is uncaused, does it follow that it is fortuitous or capricious, something that happens in the agent at random—as it were "out of the blue?" I believe it does not follow.

Suppose I perform the action of turning on my computer. It could be that I am under the power of another agent who

7. We should note that the problem of *explaining* the agent's exercise of active power is separate from the problem of whether or not she is *responsible* for that exercise of power. I say the second problem is more basic because if it should turn out that the agent can bear no responsibility for or control over her exercise of power, then the agent-causation theory of responsibility and freedom collapses immediately.

has produced in me an irresistible urge to turn on the computer. If so, then on Reid's theory my action is caused by this other agent. It remains my action, but I am passive with respect to it and am not responsible for it. Reid would allow that I am, at best, a 'necessary agent.' But let us suppose that I perform the action freely. If so then *I cause* the act of will to perform that action, the action is truly mine, and I am prima facie responsible for it. But I cause this action by exercising my active power to cause it. And since it is *active power* that is being exercised, power that includes both the power to cause and power not to cause, my exercise of active power cannot itself be caused, either by me or something else. Must it be true, then, that my exercise of active power occurs randomly, without purpose or explanation? It hardly seems right to draw this conclusion. If we are considering a type of event, an act of will, for example, that is sometimes caused by me as agent, and sometimes caused in me by irresistible forces or some other agent, and such an event suddenly occurs without any cause at all, then it seems reasonable to view its occurrence as capricious or arbitrary. But it is not as though an exercise of active power is sometimes caused by me or something else. By virtue of its very nature it cannot have a cause. Moreover, it is only by virtue of it that I as agent *can cause and be responsible for* any action or change. My claim, then, is that once we understand these things we can see that it is at least doubtful that my exercise of active power need be capricious or fortuitous. A token of an event-type that *can have a cause* may occur at random if it occurs without a cause. An event *by virtue of which* an agent does not cause some action or change may occur at random if it occurs without a cause. But an exercise of active power satisfies neither of these conditions. It cannot have a cause, and by virtue of it an agent causes and is prima facie responsible for her actions. This being so, I conclude that we lack adequate grounds for viewing the exercise of active power as a random, fortuitous event.

In addition, we can note, as Chisholm has taught us, that

lacking an event-cause does not preclude an event from having contributing causes.[8] If I exercise my active power to run a mile at noon, and this exercise of power lacks both a sufficient-causal condition (an event-cause) and an agent-cause (as I have argued it must), there still will be ever so many contributing causes to the occurrence of that exercise of power. The presence of oxygen causally contributes to the exercise of my power to run a mile, for it is a causally necessary condition of that exercise of power. (The exercise of that power logically implies that I run a mile. But the latter is causally impossible without the presence of oxygen. Therefore, the former is also causally impossible without the presence of oxygen.)

By virtue of the fact that an exercise of active power will have necessary causal conditions, it is possible for me and for you to causally contribute to a future exercise of my active power. For if you or I bring about such a necessary causal condition and I subsequently exercise that power, each of us may have contributed causally to that exercise of power. And, as Chisholm has pointed out, if my having a certain motive or reason is causally necessary for my performing some action, then you may causally influence my action by providing me with that motive or reason. For if I subsequently exercise my power to perform that act, you will have provided a necessary condition (in the form of a motive or reason) for that exercise of power.[9]

Thus, the fact that an exercise of active power lacks an efficient cause or an event-cause is far from being a conclusive reason for thinking it is completely capricious or fortuitous, a random event for which the agent has no responsibility at all. This being so, we are justified in rejecting the inference from (1) to (2) in the argument against the view that an agent may

8. See Bogdan.

9. In Bogdan (63–64), Chisholm cites additional ways of causally contributing to actions that are indetermined in the sense of lacking an event-cause (a sufficient causal condition).

be responsible for his exercise of active power even though he is not the efficient cause of it.

But it is one thing to hold that from the fact that an exercise of active power is uncaused it does not follow that the agent is not responsible for that exercise of power, and another thing to argue that the agent is responsible for that exercise of power. Can we do the latter? I think a great deal rests on this point. For unless an exercise of active power is up to the agent whose power is thus exercised, unless the agent has control over and is responsible for that exercise of active power, we will be deprived of any basis for claiming (1) that it is up to the agent whether to agent-cause her action and (2) that the agent is responsible for bringing about her action. I think we can see this with our example of my action of turning on the computer. If this action is free, then I cause the action by exercising my active power to bring it about. Indeed, it is by virtue of my exercise of that power that I cause it and am responsible for it. Now if my exercise of active power is something that simply happens to me, something that I am not responsible for, something that isn't in my control, then surely the claim that I am responsible for causing my action of turning on the computer, that it is up to me whether or not I cause it, is a claim without foundation. In short, if the agent is not responsible for his exercise of active power in bringing it about that he turns on his computer, the whole theory that builds responsibility and freedom on agent-causation turns out to be a rope of sand.

I believe it follows from the very conception of active power that an exercise of it is not only uncaused (as we've already established) but also such that it is up to the agent whose exercise it is and therefore something for which he is prima facie responsible. On the assumption that I have active power with respect to turning on my computer, we can express the argument as follows.

1. It is in my power to cause (or not cause) my action of turning on the computer (from our assumption).

therefore,
2. It is up to me whether I cause my action of turning on the computer.
3. I cause my action of turning on my computer if, and only if, I exercise my active power to turn on the computer.
therefore,
4. It is up to me whether I exercise my active power to turn on the computer.[10]

What this argument shows is that an event may be both uncaused and yet in the control of the agent in whom that event occurs. The events of which this is true resemble ordinary human actions (turning on the computer, for example) more than events that are not human actions (the beating of one's heart, for example). An exercise of active power resembles an ordinary human action in that it is something the agent does, as opposed to something that merely happens to the agent. But unlike an ordinary human action, an exercise of active power is an uncaused event. And what we've just seen is that whether the agent exercises active power to bring about a volition or action is *up to* that agent, something for which the agent is prima facie responsible. Contrary, then, to the common assumption that an uncaused event must be utterly fortuitous, not within the agent's control, just the reverse is true when that event is an exercise of active power.

With this matter behind us, we are now in a better position to examine the second set of objections to Reid's theory of libertarian freedom: those that argue that the possession of libertarian freedom would be harmful because the agent's actions would be uninfluenced by motives and therefore capricious, ungovernable, and unaffected by reward or punishment.

It is best, I believe, to focus our discussion on Reid's dispute with the necessitarians over the place and influence of

10. If it is up to me whether to exercise my active power, then if I do exercise it I am prima facie responsible for that exercise of active power.

motives in human action. The issue between them is *not* whether any important action can occur in the absence of a relevant motive or reason. As Reid himself makes clear:

> in *all* determinations of the mind that are of any importance, there must be something in the preceding state of the mind that disposes or inclines us to that determination. If the mind were always in a state of perfect indifference, without any excitement, motive, or reason, to act, or not to act, to act one way rather than another, our active power, having no end to pursue, no rule to direct its exertions, would be given in vain. We should either be altogether inactive, and never will to do anything, or our volitions would be perfectly unmeaning and futile, being neither wise nor foolish, virtuous nor vicious. (533, emphasis mine)

Necessitarians and libertarians (Reid included) do disagree as to whether *any* deliberate action can occur in the absence of a reason or motive to perform *that particular action.* Reid contends, I think rightly, that we deliberately do many "trifling actions" for which we have no conscious motive at all.[11] In addition, there are cases where an end may be achieved equally well by different actions. In such cases we have no motive that selects the particular action we perform. For example, suppose you have reason to put a quarter into a vending machine. You reach into your pocket and pull out your change: one nickel, one dime, two quarters. You then put one of the quarters into the machine. Now you had a reason to put one or the other of the quarters into the machine. But did you have a motive or reason for putting *that quarter,* rather than the other one, into the machine? Clearly, we would be hard put to say what your motive or reason was, if there was one. You had a reason to pick one of the two quarters but no

11. To the claim that in such cases the motive is unconscious, Reid replies that this is an arbitrary supposition and is tantamount to saying that I may be influenced by an argument I have never thought of (608).

reason to pick that quarter rather than the other one. (Perhaps you picked it in order to get on with the events of the day. But that reason would have been equally satisfied by your picking the other quarter.) We can say that you picked that quarter *in order to operate the vending machine.* But the same explanation would have been true had you picked the other quarter. Empirically and phenomenologically, it would seem that cases like this one must go on the libertarian side of the debate.[12] The necessitarian has a theory that precludes such cases, provided he holds that motives are the sole causes of human actions. What these cases do, at best, is to cast doubt on the view that all actions are caused solely by motives. It is open to the necessitarian to accept this conclusion, noting that in such cases as the one above the event that causes the action is something other than a motive or reason.

The second, and more serious point of disagreement between Reid and the necessitarians over the place and influence of motives in human action concerns what occurs when there is a *definite motive* for performing *a particular action.* Reid puts the necessitarian position on this issue as follows:

> When there is no motive on the other side, this motive must determine the agent: When there are contrary motives, the strongest must prevail. We reason from men's motives to their actions, as we do from other causes to their effects. If a man be a free agent, and be not governed by motives, all his actions must be mere caprice, rewards and punishments can have no effect, and such a being must be absolutely ungovernable. (608)

For our purpose, we can focus attention on cases involving a conflict of motives. According to the necessitarian, in these cases the strongest motive must prevail. The problem with this position is to provide a criterion for determining the strongest motive, independent of its success in prevailing over

12. For Reid's discussion of such cases, see p. 609.

the contrary motives. Reid grants that when the competing motives are of the same kind, it may be relatively easy to determine which is the strongest. (A bribe for a large sum of money is a stronger motive than a bribe for a small sum). "But when the motives are of different kinds—as money and fame, duty and worldly interest, health and strength, riches and honour—by what rule shall we judge which is the strongest motive?" (610).

From his discussion it is clear that Reid thinks the necessitarians have no solution to this problem that does not beg the question of motives being causes of our actions. Reid's own contribution to providing a test for the strength of a motive (independent of its prevailing) rests on his distinction (discussed in Chapter 7) between *animal motives* and *rational motives.* Animal motives are addressed to the animal part of our nature (appetites, desires, natural affections, etc.); whereas rational motives are addressed to the rational part of our nature that judges ends (judgments about our moral duty or our own good upon the whole). The crucial difference between these two sets of motives lies *in the way in which they influence us to act.* According to Reid, animal motives "give a blind impulse to the will." It is proper, accordingly, to view animal motives, like hunger, fear, etc., as *forces* that act upon our will directly, forces that, unless resisted by an equal or greater force, will impel us to act in accordance with them.

> Such animal motives give an impulse to the agent, to which he yields with ease; and if the impulse be strong, it cannot be resisted without an effort which requires a greater or less degree of self-command. The strength of motives of this kind is perceived, not by our judgment, but by our feeling; and that is the strongest of contrary motives, to which he can yield with ease, or which it requires an effort of self-command to resist; and this we may call the *animal test* of the strength of motives. (611)

Reid thinks that the strongest motive (by the animal test) always prevails in the brute animals. For he thinks they lack both rational motives and active power. "They do not appear to have any self-command; an appetite or passion in them is overcome only by a stronger contrary one. On this account, they are not accountable for their actions, nor can they be subjects of law" (611). Indeed, Reid appears to accept the necessitarian objection to free will, so far as the brute animals are concerned. Although he professes not to *know* whether they have free will (active power over the determinations of the will), he thinks that since they lack the rational motives, there would be no good purpose served by their having a power to act contrary to the strongest motive (by the animal test). "Nor do I see what end could be served by giving them a power over the determinations of their own will, unless to make them intractable by discipline, which we see they are not" (600).

The necessitarian objection to free will, briefly put, is that it would make our actions a matter of caprice, not subject to the influence of motives, rewards and punishments, etc. Reid, as we just saw, draws something like this conclusion with respect to the brute animals. If these animals enjoyed a large measure of active power over their actions, our efforts to influence their behavior, to train them, etc., by providing them with motives, by rewarding and punishing them, etc., may have little chance of success—certainly less chance of success than if they have no such power, their actions being causally determined by motives, rewards, punishments, and the like.

What, then, does Reid see as the *value* of free will on the human level? For what purpose did nature (or God) provide us with active power over our wills, granted that nature (or God) does nothing in vain? To appreciate the answer to this question, we need to look again at the rational motives to action and the test by which their *strength* is to be determined.

As we noted in our study of rational self-love and duty (Chapter 7), these motives, according to Reid, do not directly incite or impel the will. They are felt by us not as forces impelling us to act but as judgments about what is our long-range good or what is our duty. Since we are so constituted as to value or view with esteem the person who acts out of regard for duty or her good upon the whole, we have some desire to so act ourselves. But, in general, it takes little in the way of effort to avoid doing what duty alone (or our good upon the whole) requires, as opposed to the difficulty we have resisting the demands of our appetites, desires, and natural affections. In fact, the two sets of motives (animal and rational) influence us in such different ways that Reid proposes a quite different test for measuring the strength of a rational motive. Speaking of the rational motives, he remarks:

> They do not give a blind impulse to the will, as animal motives do. They convince, but they do not impel, unless as may often happen, they excite some passion of hope, or fear, or desire. Such passions may be excited by conviction, and may operate in its aid as other animal motives do. But there may be conviction without passion; and the conviction of what we ought to do, in order to some end which we have judged fit to be pursued, is what I call a rational motive.
>
> If there be any competition between rational motives, it is evident that the strongest, in the eye of reason, is that which it is most our duty and our real happiness to follow. Our duty and our real happiness are ends which are inseparable; and they are the ends which every man, endowed with reason, is conscious he ought to pursue in preference to all others. This we may call the *rational test* of the strength of motives. A motive which is the strongest, according to the animal test, may be, and very often is, the weakest according to the rational.
>
> The grand and the important competition of contrary motives is between the animal, on the one hand, and the rational on the other. This is the conflict between the flesh and the spirit, upon the event of which the character of men depends.
>
> If it be asked, Which of these is the strongest motive? The answer is, That the first is commonly strongest, when they are tried by the animal test. If it were not so, human life would be no state of trial. It would not be a warfare, nor would virtue require any effort or self-command. No man would have any

> temptation to do wrong. But, when we try the contrary motives by the rational test, it is evident that the rational motive is always the strongest.
>
> And now, I think, it appears, that the strongest motive, according to either of the tests I have mentioned, does not always prevail.
>
> In every wise and virtuous action, the motive that prevails is the strongest according to the rational test, but commonly the weakest according to the animal. In every foolish and in every vicious action, the motive that prevails is commonly the strongest according to the animal test, but always the weakest according to the rational test. (611–12)

I've quoted Reid at length here for two reasons. First, to make clear his rational test of strength, so that we can understand why, in a conflict between animal and rational motives, the former are almost always the strongest by the animal test but never the strongest by the rational test. Second, to enable us to see what nature's (or God's) purpose was in providing rational beings (beings with rational motives) with active power over the will. For, clearly, if we have no power to resist a force acting directly on our will, then in a contest between animal and rational motives, the animal must always win. The purpose of free will, of active power over the determinations of the will, is to *enable us* to act the better part, to cast our lot with duty or rational self-love, to do what we ought or what is wisest, as opposed to yielding to the forces exerted on the will by our passions. The gift of free will, however, is a double-edged sword. When we use it properly and follow the calm voice of duty, resisting the gale of the passions, we are fit subjects for moral praise and esteem. When, however, we use it badly, giving way to passion even though we have the power to resist, failing to follow the call of duty or rational self-love, we act immorally or foolishly and are subject to blame and condemnation—judgments inapplicable to beings lacking free will.

Our brief study of Reid's view of the place and influence of motives in human action has brought four points to the surface.

1. Most significant human actions are preceded by something in the preceding state of mind that disposes or inclines us to perform that action.
2. Animal motives are forces that act directly on the will. They impel the will to action unless resisted by an equal or stronger force.
3. Rational motives do not impel the will; they are felt as advice. Their influence is upon our judgment, by producing a belief that a certain act is our duty or conducive to our good upon the whole.
4. The purpose of active power over the determinations of the will is to enable the agent to resist the force of the animal motives in favor of the judgments of the rational motives.

Do these points amount to an adequate response to the second set of necessitarian objections? At one level, I believe they do. What is not so clear, however, is whether Reid's response, while answering the objections at one level, doesn't do so at the cost of permitting the same objections to appear again at a deeper level in his theory.

It should be obvious from Reid's remarks that free will is not inconsistent with the view that motives *influence* us in the performance of our actions. Clearly, so far as the animal motives are concerned, Reid's view is that a person who has such a motive is subject to its force upon the will *whether or not the will is free.* Other things being equal, hunger has the same degree of force upon the will of a person who lacks free will as it does on a person who has free will. If we suppose that the degree of active power the agent possesses is sufficient to resist the force brought upon the will by the state of hunger, then if the person exercises that power, the agent's volition will not be what it would have been had that power not existed or not been exercised. But while Reid thinks we perform many trifling actions without having any motives to do them, his general view is that we seldom use our active power to *overcome* the force of an animal motive when we have no conflicting animal or rational motive. So the picture his theory presents does not at all conflict with the view that motives influence our volitions and actions.

Does Reid's theory permit that motives may influence the will and our actions by virtue of *causing* the occurrence of a volition to perform a certain action? Reid's official answer to this question is no. Motives are not causes, because they are not beings endowed with active power (608). After making this point—which is surely correct—Reid continues: "Motives, therefore, may *influence* to action, but they do not act. They may be compared to advice, or exhortation, which leaves a man still at liberty. For in vain is advice given when there is not a power either to do or to forbear what it recommends. In like manner, motives suppose liberty in the agent, otherwise they have no influence at all" (608–9). This passage is puzzling in the light of our discussion of animal motives. The passage makes good sense *provided* Reid is restricting the discussion to rational motives. And I can only suppose he intended to be doing that, although the passage occurs within a context in which it is clear that motives in general are being discussed. Be this as it may, I think Reid's position *should be* that (1) no motive can be an efficient cause (agent-cause) of a volition, (2) animal motives on occasion may be event-causes of volitions, and (3) no rational motive (*qua* rational motive) can be an event-cause of a volition.

I take it that Reid's own view is (or should be) that animal motives do function as event-causes (physical causes) in the brute animals. Moreover, when an animal motive occurs in a human agent in circumstances where no contrary motives are of equal force, then, providing the motive and the circumstances are causally sufficient for the agent's lacking sufficient active power to overcome the force of that animal motive, I see no reason why that motive should not be viewed as the event-cause of the ensuing volition. Suppose, however, that the agent does possess sufficient active power to balance or overcome the stronger animal motive. If the agent exercises that power, then the animal motive will not be followed by the volition that would have occurred in those circumstances had the agent lacked that active power. Suppose, then, that the agent does not exercise that active power. Is the animal motive the event-cause of the volition that then occurs? I should think not. The animal motive may well have been causally necessary for the occurrence of that volition. For although the agent had power to cause the nonoccurrence of that volition, being unaided by any motive he may not have had sufficient power to bring the volition about.[13] But the motive and the actual circumstances that obtained were not causally sufficient for the occurrence of that volition. If the motive reached its intensity at t and the volition to act from the motive occurred at t + 2, it will not be true that at t an event obtained (a complex conjunctive event) such that, given that event, the occurrence of the volition at t + 2 was physically necessary. For at t + 1 the agent had the active power to overcome the force of that motive on the will. Thus at t there was no event causally sufficient for the occurrence of the volition at t + 2.

Although Reid has no theory worked out concerning *partial causes,* various remarks he makes suggest that if an agent had power to overcome an animal motive and did not exercise that power, he is to be viewed as in part responsible for, if not a partial cause of, the volition and action prompted by that motive. Thus, for example, he remarks: "In actions that proceed from appetite or passion, we are passive in part, and

13. It is important to recall here that power to cause A does not entail power to cause non-A; it entails power *not* to cause A. Similarly, power to cause non-A does not entail power to cause A; it entails power *not* to cause non-A.

only in part active. They are therefore partly imputed to the passion; and if it is supposed to be irresistible, we do not impute them to the man at all" (534). The cases that particularly concern him are those in which some animal motive (a sudden wave of fear, for example) exerts considerable force on the will to initiate an action that is in opposition to a rational motive concerning our duty. For when the force exerted on the will is slight, Reid regards the agent as fully responsible for failing in his duty. And when the force is genuinely regarded as irresistible, as stronger than the agent's power over his will, then the agent is no cause at all and is not morally responsible for his volition and action. But when the agent could have prevented the volition by exerting a considerable degree of power and fails to exert that degree of power, the agent may be regarded as a partial cause of the volition. For what he freely fails to do (prevent the volition) is a necessary condition of the volition's occurrence. In any case, Reid clearly thinks that in such a case the volition is to be *attributed* partly to the agent and partly to his animal motive.

Thus far I've sought to defend Reid against a variety of charges arising from what has emerged as a fundamental point in his theory of freedom: *the agent's exercise of active power is an event that has no agent-cause and no event-cause.* It has been charged that such a view leaves exercises of active power as (1) events over which the agent has no control or responsibility and (2) as acts utterly uninfluenced by motives and therefore as capricious, and unaffected by reward or punishment. I have argued that neither of these charges is really successful against Reid's theory. Moreover, I've argued that there are compelling reasons for the view that the agent has control over and is responsible for his exercises of active power. I've also tried to show how Reid's theory does provide for the influence of motives in human action. Earlier, however, I noted that while Reid seems to succeed at one level in answering the charge that free agents cannot be influenced by motives, he may do so at the price of permitting, if not requiring, that the charge be raised at a deeper level in his agent-causation theory of freedom. I will bring this study to a close by considering this problem, which, in honor of Leibniz, I will call "Leibniz's Queen Objection."

Leibniz pictures libertarian theories as viewing the will as a queen who decides whether to listen to her ministers (the understanding) or to her favorite ladies-in-waiting (the passions), sometimes listening to one or both, sometimes listening to neither, but in the end taking their advice or not as seems good to her. This won't do as an accurate picture of Reid's theory, for Reid doesn't view the will as a substance that takes advice or makes decisions. (It is the person, not the will, that listens to advice and makes decisions. The will is the power a person has to make various decisions, to determine the mind by producing volitions.) But something close to Leibniz's picture is endorsed by Reid. In place of the queen, Reid proposes the picture of the judge. In place of ministers and courtiers, Reid pictures competing motives as lawyers pleading opposite sides of a case before the judge. The point of the picture, in both Leibniz and Reid, is to drive home the point that the motives do not compel the outcome. It is the queen or judge that has power over the outcome.

> Contrary motives may very properly be compared to advocates pleading the opposite sides of a cause at the bar. It would be very weak reasoning to say, that such an advocate is the most powerful pleader, because sentence was given on his side. The sentence is in the power of the judge, not of the advocate. It is equally weak reasoning, in proof of necessity, to say, such a motive prevailed, therefore it is the strongest; since the defenders of liberty maintain that the determination was made by the man, and not by the motive. (611)

The problem evoked by the image of the person as a queen or a judge in relation to the motives, whether animal or rational, that plead opposite sides of a cause is that in order to choose to act in accordance with one motive rather than another the queen or judge will need some reason or motive (second-order) for preferring one first-order motive over another first-order motive. If this isn't so, then we must envisage the person as having no basis whatever for preferring one first-order motive over another. This might not cause intellectual difficulty if the first-order motives are both animal and the one acted upon is the strongest according to the animal test. But suppose the person acts in accordance with the weaker animal motive. Or suppose there is a motive on one side only, and the person acts against this motive. Is this some random exertion of active power, without any reason or motive at all? Reid reminds us that sometimes human beings are willful, obstinate, or capricious. His point is that sometimes we may act against the only motive, or against the strongest motive, simply out of capriciousness. But such cases as these don't fit the image of a judge exercising thought and judgment in giving the nod to one motive over another. Surely the man (judge) is not being capricious. In his note on this passage, Hamilton raises the right question: "But was the *man* determined by no motive to that determination? Was his specific volition to this or to that without a cause?" (611).

We explain the agent's choices by her motives, both animal and rational. If the agent uses her active power to overcome the force of the animal motives in favor of the call of duty, on Reid's theory we cannot say that the rational motive and the circumstances necessitated the agent to choose as she did. For that would preclude any exercise of active power; it would mean that our agent did not choose freely. This appears to lead directly to the view of the agent as a queen or judge, freely choosing to act from one of the competing motives. But then our problem of explanation resurfaces at a deeper level in Reid's theory: the level of the agent's selection of the motive by which we had hoped to explain the agent's action. Why, on this occasion, did our agent favor her rational motive for doing A over her animal motive for doing B?

The explanation problem can be put quite simply in terms of questions and answers.

1. Why did the person exercise her active power to do A?
2. Because the agent had motive M to do A and motive M′ not to do A, and she acted from motive M.
3. Did motive M necessitate the person's exercise of active power in doing A?
4. Of course not. It is logically impossible for any motive to necessitate the agent's exercise of active power in doing A.
5. Why then did the agent exercise her active power in choosing to act from M rather than from M′?
6. Well, I suppose the agent must have had some motive M* for choosing to act from M rather than from M′.
7. . . .

As with our earlier problem of what, if anything, causes an exercise of active power, I cannot find any significant discussion of this problem of explanation in Reid's writings. Perhaps the closest we come is in the following important set of remarks in defense of the libertarian theory concerning the influence of motives. Because of their general importance, I quote Reid at length.

> It is true that we reason from men's motives to their actions, and in many cases, with great probability, but never with absolute certainty. And to infer from this, that men are necessarily determined by motives, is very weak reasoning.
>
> For let us suppose, for a moment, that men have moral liberty, I would ask, what use may they be expected to make of this liberty? It may surely be expected that, of the various actions within the sphere of their power, they will choose what pleases them most for the present, or what appears to be most for their real, though distant good. When there is a competition between these motives, the foolish will prefer present gratification; the wise the greater and more distant good.
>
> Now, is not this the very way in which we see men at? Is it not from the presumption that they act in this way, that we reason

> from their motives to their actions? Surely it is. Is it not weak reasoning, therefore, to argue, that men have not liberty, because they act in that very way in which they would act if they had liberty? It would surely be more like reasoning to draw the contrary conclusions from the same premises.
>
> Nor is it better reasoning to conclude that, if men are not necessarily determined by motives, all their actions must be capricious.
>
> To resist the strongest animal motives when duty requires, is so far from being capricious that it is, in the highest degree, wise and virtuous. And we hope this is often done by good men.
>
> To act against rational motives, must always be foolish, vicious, or capricious. And, it cannot be denied that there are too many such actions done. But is it reasonable to conclude, that, because liberty may be abused by the foolish, and the vicious, therefore it can never be put to its proper use, which is to act wisely and virtuously? (612)

On the basis of this passage, I suggest the following as a possible Reidian reply to the apparent regress of explanations generated by Leibniz's Queen Objection. We need to distinguish an agent's *character* from *particular motives* the agent has for specific actions. We can imagine two people in similar circumstances confronted by roughly the same motives for action. The one acts from the motive of duty. The other acts against duty in favor of the gratification of some immediate desire. If we suppose that each action is performed freely, we then encounter the explanation problem: Why does the one person freely act from the motive of duty? Why does the other person freely act from the motive of immediate gratification? The image of the queen or judge is misleading because (1) it leads us to look for some second-order motive by which the person selects between the competing first-order motives and (2) it encourages us to believe that in addition to the first-order action of acting from the motive of duty (or immediate gratification), there is a second-level action of choosing to act from this or that first-order motive. Perhaps

Reid's real view is the following. In addition to the particular motives confronting the agent, there is the agent's character: some more or less well-developed set of dispositions to act from a regard for duty and one's good upon the whole or from one's animal appetites, desires, and affections. When the motives and the circumstances are roughly the same, it is to the *characters* of the agents that we turn to explain why the motive of duty prevailed in the one and why the motive of immediate gratification prevailed in the other. As Reid remarks: "When there is a competition between these motives, the *foolish* will prefer present gratification; the *wise* the greater and more distant good" (612, emphasis mine). Of course, the combination of character, motive, and circumstances does not necessitate the action. Even the steady person of good character may act out of character. But the *influence* that particular motives have in our free actions is shaped in part by the character of the person who is subject to those motives.

Whether the above suggestion can be adequately developed to solve the explanation problem is a matter that lies beyond the scope of this study. Of course, if by an *explanation* of the agent's action we mean some complex prior event or state including motives, character, and circumstances that is *causally sufficient* for the agent's action, this simply begs the question against there being any explanation in Reid's theory for a free action. In place of a deterministic explanation, we must substitute a probabilistic explanation of an agent's free actions. Probabilistic explanations of an agent's future actions are constantly given by all of us. If these actions are genuinely free in the libertarian sense, such explanations are ultimate; they are not temporary substitutes for deterministic explanations that await further knowledge of the state of the agent and the world prior to his free action. But the fact that Reid's theory of the relations of motives to free actions provides for probabilistic explanation suffices to put to rest the necessitarian charge that libertarian free actions are fortuitous because they are uninfluenced by motives.

Editions Cited

Aquinas, Thomas. *Summa Theologica*. 60 vols. Ed. Thomas Gilby. New York: McGraw-Hill, 1964.

Aristotle. *The Complete Works of Aristotle*. 2 vols. Ed. Jonathan Barnes. Princeton: Princeton University Press, 1984.

Butler, Joseph. *Fifteen Sermons*. London, 1726.

Clarke, Samuel. *A Discourse Concerning the Being and Attributes of God, the Obligations of Natural Religion, and the Truth and Certainty of the Christian Revelation*. 9th ed. London, 1738.

——. *The Works*. 1738. Reprinted in 4 vols. by Garland Publishing, 1978.

Collins, Anthony. *Determinism and Freewill: Anthony Collins' A Philosophical Inquiry Concerning Human Liberty*. Ed. J. O'Higgins. The Hague: Martinus Nijhoff, 1976.

Edwards, Jonathan. *Freedom of the Will*. Ed. Paul Ramsey. New Haven: Yale University Press, 1957.

Hobbes, Thomas. *The English Works of Thomas Hobbes*. London, 1841.

Hume, David. *A Treatise of Human Nature*. 2d ed. Ed. Peter H. Nidditch. Oxford: Oxford University Press, 1978.

Kant, Immanuel. *Critique of Practical Reason*. Trans. Lewis W. Beck. Indianapolis: Bobbs-Merrill, 1956.

King, William. *An Essay on the Origin of Evil.* 2d ed. Translated from the Latin with Notes by Edmund Law. London, 1732.

Leibniz, G. W. *Theodicy.* Trans. E. M. Huggard, ed. Austin Farrer. La Salle, Ill.: Open Court, 1985.

——. *New Essays on Human Understanding.* Trans. and ed. P. Remnant and J. Bennett. Cambridge: Cambridge University Press, 1982.

Locke, John. *An Essay Concerning Human Understanding.* Ed. Peter H. Nidditch. 1975. Oxford: Oxford University Press, 1979.

Reid, Thomas. *The Works of Thomas Reid, D.D.* 8th ed. Ed. Sir William Hamilton. Edinburgh, 1895. [Reprint. With an introduction by H. M. Bracken. Hildesheim: Georg Olms Verlag, 1983.]

Index

Library of Congress Cataloging-in-Publication Data

Rowe, William L., 1931–
Thomas Reid on freedom and morality / William L. Rowe.
p. cm.
Includes index.
ISBN 0-8014-2557-3 (alk. paper)
1. Liberty—History—18th century. 2. Ethics, Modern—18th century. 3. Reid, Thomas, 1710–1796. I. Title.
B1538.R68 1991
123′.5′092—dc20 90-55715